The Disciple

The Disciple

On Becoming Truly Human

LUCY PEPPIATT

 CASCADE *Books* · Eugene, Oregon

THE DISCIPLE
On Becoming Truly Human

Cascade Books
An Imprint of Wipf and Stock Publishers
199 W. 8th Ave., Suite 3
Eugene, OR 97401

www.wipfandstock.com

ISBN 13: 978-1-61097-984-9

Cataloging-in-Publication data:

Peppiatt, Lucy.

    The disciple: on becoming truly human / Lucy Peppiatt.

    xvi + 154 p. ; 23 cm—Includes bibliographical references and index.

    ISBN 13: 978-1-61097-984-9

    1. Discipling (Christianity). 2. Spiritual formation—Christianity. 3. Sanctification—Christianity. 4. Trinity. I. Title.

BV4520 P362 2012

Manufactured in the USA.

For Nick, Seth, Harry, Roscoe, Jem, Jon, and Jules

Contents

Foreword

THERE IS AN ANCIENT practice of the church that has now been largely lost, at least in the form it once took. That practice is catechesis, the practice of forming disciples of Jesus Christ in preparation for baptism and equipping them for a life of discipleship following their first profession of faith. Typically, in the Western church the practice of forming disciples tends to take place in a less structured and more haphazard way than it once did. That lack of structure and discipline reflects the proclivities of Western culture. People today are inclined toward a more open-ended, less doctrinally prescriptive, and more self-directed investigation of religious faith, or of "spirituality" as some choose to call it, often indicating thereby a preference for a spiritual journey tailored to the "needs" and predilections of the individual explorer. The ready-made answers of traditional catechisms do not suit this mood. There may be some benefits deriving from these cultural preferences but there are also some very considerable losses including in particular, the widespread biblical and theological illiteracy among many church-goers today, a reduced capacity to think Christianly about all aspects of human life and therefore to follow Christ in all spheres of life, and a lack of confidence in evangelism, reflecting a widespread incapacity to give a coherent account of the hope that is within us.

This book, written by Lucy Peppiatt, is not a course of catechetical instruction in the old sense, but it may be located in the space left vacant by the demise of formal catechesis. What is written here is directed toward the formation of Christian disciples, of those new to the faith and of those who are some distance down the road and who, like all of us, struggle sometimes with the demands of faith. This is a wise book. Its wisdom is founded in part upon the formal training in theology that Lucy has done, including a PhD thesis on Spirit Christology and mission. But it shows forth as well a wisdom gained through Lucy's own journey of discipleship and through her vast experience of accompanying and nurturing others in faith. Lucy, along with her husband Nick, have worked together in ministry in Zimbabwe, in Sheffield, and now in Bristol, where they have established a church community directed especially toward ministry among those who are just setting out as disciples of Jesus. It is from that context this book has emerged.

Lucy likens the life of discipleship to an apprenticeship. It is a fruitful image, for an apprentice is one who is being inducted through instruction, imitation, and participation into a particular set of practices, in this case the practices of faith taught and perfected by Christ and enabled by the Holy Spirit. Of course, in the case of Christian discipleship, the apprenticeship is a lifelong one. There will never be a time when we are ready to take leave of the Master. Rather, our apprenticeship matures precisely as we are drawn more and more to participate in his life and are conformed to his likeness.

Lucy's account of discipleship is characterised by its emphasis upon the deep joy of a life lived "in Christ." It is an account written, however, by someone who knows that the way of faith passes through the wilderness, that there are Gethsemanes to be faced where discernment of the will of God is far from straightforward, and where obedience is a matter of costly sacrifice. Yet Lucy provides encouragement that, amidst these challenges of faith, we are never without the loving care of the Father, the companionship of Jesus and the sustaining, comforting, and empowering presence of God's Spirit. This account of Christian discipleship is, above all, therefore, a testimony to the sufficiency of God's grace. I warmly commend it to you.

Murray Rae
University of Otago, New Zealand

Acknowledgments

IT IS ACTUALLY IMPOSSIBLE to acknowledge the many people who have been involved in the formation of a book, especially a book on the shaping of a Christian life within communities. Over the years there have been hundreds of people who have contributed to my reflections on this topic. I am so grateful to so many for their wisdom, insights, encouragement, and friendship. There are some who stand out, however, for taking a special part, in some way, in the shaping of this project, and for that I am especially grateful. To start at the beginning, I would like to thank Simon Downham for encouraging me to pursue academic theology and for advising me to go to King's College, London to do so. I trusted his judgment and this was to start me on a journey that was genuinely life-changing. My theologian friends have added to my life in so many ways. They challenge my ideas, encourage me, and most importantly, make me laugh. For great friendship, fantastic conversations, for encouraging me to write in general, and for reassuring me that theology and worship go hand in hand, I would like to thank especially Oliver Crisp, Gavin D'Costa, Lindsey Hall, Alan Spence, and Jonathan Chan. From my King's days, my special thanks goes to Nabil Shehadi who, years later on a trip from Bristol to Shepton Mallet, suggested I turn a talk into this book. In the planning of the book, I am deeply grateful to Simon Ponsonby, who helped me with my initial proposals, and has supported me every step of the way. My readers, Seth Crawley, Bruce Podmore, and Julian Springer all gave me invaluable feedback. I am so grateful for the time and the effort they all put in.

Acknowledgments

Because this is a book about learning to follow Jesus in all and every circumstance and relationship, I would really like to thank my family I grew up with, including my siblings, cousins, my two aunts, and my uncle, and in later years, the family I married into. They have shaped me and formed me and I love them so much for being godly, prayerful, sometimes difficult, funny, and naughty, all at once. Most importantly, I want to thank my parents, Hugh and Claire Peppiatt, for being so incredibly easy to honor, and for loving me in such a way that, through them, I learned about the deep and unconditional love of God, and the freedom of the Christian life. As well as gratitude for my own family, I am so grateful for all the communities and churches that have been my extended family over the years: for the people who have studied the Bible with me; for all the people who have lived with us; and for the people who have worked with me and prayed with me. I would also like to thank my close friends so very much, who have "borne" with me through thick and thin. They know what they mean to me. It is with all these people that my thinking and practices have been forged.

In everything, I am especially indebted to Murray Rae, for whom I reserve a particular expression of gratitude. It is really true to say that without his encouragement a few years ago to embark on a PhD in theology, this book would never even have been contemplated, let alone written. I have been hugely privileged to have had a PhD supervisor, a theological mentor, and a friend of such integrity. His careful advice, continuing encouragement, and insightful questioning makes anything I write far, far better than it would have been without him. Needless to say, he does not always agree with everything I write, and any shortcomings left in the finished product are my own.

Finally, and most importantly, my deepest gratitude goes to my husband, Nick Crawley, and to our four sons, Seth, Harry, Roscoe, and Jem. Living with growing boys has been one of the greatest joys of my life. Their teasing, irreverence, annoying habits, questions, honesty, freedom in worship, and faith are some of the most unquantifiably precious gifts to us as parents. They have taught me so much about God and life, and are my favorite people in the world to hang out with. Nick's deep love and knowledge of Scripture, and his commitment to pray has shaped our family, and given us all so much. We love him for it. His endless patience in reading my work, talking and talking at ridiculous hours, and giving me time and space to pursue the things I love, is amazing. Every part of this book is shared with him.

Introduction

DO CHURCHES MAKE DISCIPLES?

IT IS NOW COMMONPLACE to hear church leaders and theologians in the West calling for a renewed focus on "discipleship." There appears to be a corporate sense that the church has failed in some way in this area, and many are concerned that we recapture the truth that discipleship is at the heart of the gospel. Matthew's Gospel ends on what we call The Great Commission. Jesus commissions his own disciples to "Go!" so that they can make disciples of others, teaching them to obey Jesus and baptizing them in the name of the Father, the Son, and the Holy Spirit. The task of the Christian is not simply to tell people the truth about Jesus, but to teach others how to love him, follow him, learn from him, and obey him. This is the heart of what it means to love God, and will be the key to learning how to love one another.

Why are Christians speaking about a "crisis" of discipleship? What is this crisis? It is not as if we have had no good models of discipleship in any of our churches. There have been thousands of committed and wonderful Christians teaching and modeling how to follow Jesus in the West in the last decades. Is it because we have lost this as our primary focus? Are church leaders working hard to make "converts" and then assuming new Christians will just get on with it? Or are we just trying to make people into "churchgoers" so that we bump up our numbers? Are we too fearful, too apathetic or too busy in our culture to give ourselves to a life of discipleship and to embrace the gift that is being offered? Or do we think the models of discipleship we have been offered are unrealistic for our own lives and circumstances, and so we have just given up? Do we have a culture in our churches of "making disciples" or are we a bit lost as to what Christian discipleship is and how it might be developed and nurtured? Whatever the reasons for this crisis, the issue before us now is how to address this problem.

For over two decades, I have worked in our churches as a lay minister alongside my husband, Nick, who is ordained. Over the years, and in many different contexts, we have wrestled with this question of what it means to be a disciple of Jesus. The questions we have revisited time and time again are, "How do we grow in this for ourselves, and how do we enable others to do so also?" Many years ago, I read a book by Dallas Willard called *The Divine Conspiracy*. I immediately loved this book on discipleship, mainly because Willard has captured something that lies at the heart of what it means to follow Jesus. Christian discipleship is not about a set of rules and propositions, but is about *being captivated by a person*. And as Willard brings out so well, Jesus is captivating and compelling. He is fascinating, challenging, brilliant, witty, subversive, joyful, full of compassion, love, and power. Moreover, he is on the side of those in life who feel they have completely missed the boat when it comes to being "spiritual," "religious," or "respectable." He is full of grace and compassion, and the only prerequisite to an effective life of discipleship is to know we are the spiritually poor. This is precisely the hope we have—in this extraordinary man Jesus, God has come to us to save us and transform us, and this is a free gift offered to all, *especially* for those who feel they could never "make it" in the religious world.

It was in this book, years ago, that I read this: "How to combine faith with obedience is surely the essential task of the church as it enters the twenty-first century."[1] I could not have agreed more. This book is an attempt, in a small way, to contribute to the furthering of that task. Once we have encountered this man Jesus and once we have heard this gospel of grace, this message of hope for the hopeless, how do we follow him in the way that he asks us to?

THINKING ABOUT DISCIPLESHIP

If we do feel we have lost the art of discipleship, what are the first steps to recovering a culture in our churches that is energized by the great

1. Willard, *The Divine Conspiracy*, 157.

commission? One of the tasks before us, as a church, is not simply to think about what we might "do" in order to become better disciples, although that is a pressing question. We might be concerned we are facing a crisis in our practices of discipleship. However, all crises of practice in the church exist because we have first had a crisis in our thinking. In order to renew our practices, we need to re-examine our thinking, our theology of discipleship. If what we are doing is not making disciples, then the first question is not, "What are we doing wrong?" but "Why are we doing what we are doing?" In other words, which biblical truths are underpinning our current practices, and what might we be missing? What has happened in our understanding of the nature of God and the nature of the Christian life that has caused us to abandon discipleship as our primary focus? What matters now, therefore, is not just that we bring the question of discipleship to the fore, but that we think and speak about discipleship in a way that is true to the nature of God and true to the Scriptures. What do we know about God's nature that tells us about the life of discipleship? What do we know of the life and teachings of Jesus that illumines the truth of discipleship? What can we discover and re-discover in the church for our generation that will lead us to believe a life of effective discipleship is not just achievable, but desirable, attractive, fulfilling, and freeing? What will give us the hope and the ability to move towards this goal and to press on to what lies ahead? This book is an attempt to answer some of those questions.

I spend my time both studying and teaching theology, and being a pastor in a local church. What this means in practice is that ideas and real life simply have to come together. From studying theology I have experienced how good theology leads people to dedicate their lives to God in deeper and more genuine and heartfelt ways. It is a catalyst for worship, praise, prayer, and mission. When we encounter really good theology, we cannot help but respond to God by offering our lives to him all over again, because we are confronted with the truth about him in fresh and powerful ways. I have also learned that our experiences of God in prayer, in worship, and through the lives of others, often unsettle our theology. When we experience God as a living presence in the person of Jesus and the power of the Spirit, we are unable to settle into a theological rut. We have to admit we are on a journey of discovery towards God. Theologians do not have all the answers, as every good theologian knows. All Christians everywhere need to be prepared to be surprised and unsettled by God.

The church needs theologians, and theologians need the church, because thinking and practice must come together and stay together. It is from this perspective that I have written this book on discipleship. In one sense, this book offers a theology of discipleship that is rooted in the Word and the Spirit, but it is my hope this will, in turn, lead to a practical response. As I have tried to articulate some of the key theological issues in relation to discipleship, I have also included some ideas for a practical response in each chapter. These are merely suggestions, but they are also there to serve as reminders that ideas about discipleship should never just remain in the realm of ideas. Being a disciple of Jesus is about lives lived in the real world of everyday life. The greatest challenge all Christians face is, how does faith work itself out in obedience? How do we become the wise men and women who learn to put Jesus's words into practice?

Having had the privilege of exploring this question with so many wonderful and inspiring people over the years, this book is just my attempt to answer that question from my own somewhat limited perspective. All I would hope is that it might serve to inspire someone to dedicate her or his life to Jesus more, and in doing this to experience the freedom and the fullness of life that is ours when we follow him, and as a result of that, to go and show others the same.

one

Laying the Foundations

APPRENTICES OF JESUS

DISCIPLE IS A WORD that really means "follower," so if we are to be and to make disciples of Jesus Christ, then we have to learn to follow him in order to enable others also to become followers. Another word for disciple is "apprentice." David Parker, a Vineyard pastor, teaches that a "disciple is more than a student, more than a member of an entourage. A disciple is an apprentice of the family business." An apprentice is a learner, a novice, or a pupil who agrees to learn from a master craftsman or an artisan, somebody skilled at what they do. When we become Christians, we all become apprentices to Jesus Christ. He is the master, and we are the learners. When we become part of the body of Christ, we also learn from one another. We can learn from those who have learned more than us, and become their apprentices as well. All of us should be following others, and have those who are following us. We should all be both teachers and students, apprentices and artisans. However, with Jesus, we are not just learning how to "do" what he does, we are learning how to be like him. It is not only skills that we are picking up, but it is that we are transformed on the inside to have his character and his mind as well.

THE GOAL OF THE CHRISTIAN LIFE

There are not that many of us who would be comfortable describing our-selves as "being like Jesus," or even "being a *bit* like Jesus." Being Christlike is not something most of us feel we excel at, let alone do moderately well. We might be happy to call ourselves Christians, but we would probably hesitate to call ourselves "good" Christians. We are, however, on occasion, happy to say that of others. We meet people who seem to us to resemble Jesus in some way, and we admire them, and even wish we could become more like them. We often have spiritual "heroes" and "heroines," either saints from the past or people whose lives we would like to emulate. The problem for most of us, though, is that when we compare our lives (and the lives of the people in our church!) to the perfect life of Jesus, there just seems to be no comparison. We fail miserably to reach the standard. But is that the picture of the Christian life that is painted for us in the Bible? Jesus teaches his disciples that they should "be holy" just as our Father in heaven is holy. Some translations say, "Be perfect, therefore, as your heavenly Fa-ther is perfect" (Matt 5:48). The idea that our lives should be Christlike is not a pattern just for exceptional Christians—those who appear to be naturally a little bit more holy than the rest of us—but for *all* believers. One of the most encouraging things is that the Bible is clear that the process of becoming like Jesus is a work of God in the lives of all believers. Christians *will* be like Jesus in the next life (1 John 3:1–3), *can* be like Jesus in this life (1 Thess 1:6–8), and *are* being made to look like him even now. Paul writes this: "And we, who with unveiled faces all reflect the Lord's glory, *are being transformed* into his likeness with ever increasing glory, which comes from the Lord, who is the Spirit" (2 Cor 3:18).

All the writers of the New Testament epistles are confident in this process of transformation. Paul is so confident that God is at work in this way in him that he exhorts the Corinthians to become not only imitators of Christ, but imitators of himself (1 Cor 4:16; 11:1). In fact, it is a theme in Paul's writings that those under his pastoral care should imitate him and follow his example, as he imitates Christ (Phil 3:17; 1 Thess 1:6; 2 Thess 3:7–9). Paul's portrayal of himself is fascinating, and seemingly paradoxi-cal. At times we see evidence of a remarkable humility in his writing, even to the point where he seems to think he has very little to recommend him. He is acutely aware of his own weaknesses and his inability to achieve any-thing apart from Christ. At other times, however, he expresses a supreme confidence in the reality that he is able to reflect Christ to those around him. Paul understands more than anyone that it is only through God's grace he is the person he is. His claim to Christlikeness, therefore, is not boastful, but entirely the opposite. It is by grace, and not by merit, that we are saved, and by grace, and not by merit, that we are transformed. God forms us into the image of his Son so that we can represent him here on earth. The early church fathers took up this idea in their teachings and writings as they addressed the question of why the eternal Son of God had to become man. Many of the fathers taught that the Son took on frail humanity, not only to forgive us of our sins and to redeem us, but in order to transform humanity, so that we could become "partakers of the divine nature" (2 Pet 1:4). Athanasius taught that Jesus became as we are, so we could become like him. Irenaeus taught that Jesus was the Son of man, "in order that man in turn might become a son of God."

There is something profoundly right and good about the notion of becoming like Christ in our own lives. The difficulty is that there is often a vast gap between the biblical truths and our real lives lived in real circumstances here on earth. When things are going well, when we have been particularly kind, righteous, or forgiving, we might feel there is a glimmer of hope. We might dare to think we are making some progress. But when life is tough, when we can no longer pray, when we lose our tempers, act selfishly, want revenge, or even "go off the rails," the reality of becoming like Jesus seems more like an illusion. When we are under pressure, we may feel as far away from being Christlike as possible. Sometimes, the more we feel we are failing, the more we hide from our friends, and the worse our situation becomes. Feelings of failure in the Christian life can be disastrous, alienating us from the church and from God. One of the reasons this happens is because we lose sight of the goal of our faith, and how this goal is going to be achieved in us. The tragedy is that having been justified by faith and saved by grace, we quickly slip back into believing that becoming like Jesus is something *we* must now work to achieve. This, of course, is a hopeless task. It will lead to feelings of failure that will eventually cause us to abandon the whole pursuit. The Christian life is one characterized by a dynamic progression. We do not stand still: we follow, seek, go, move, grow, bear fruit, and reproduce. We press on towards a prize. The confession of Jesus as Lord and Savior is not the goal or the end of the Christian life—that is only the beginning. The goal of the Christian life is to become like the Savior. We will only press on, however, when we remember that we are always simply cooperating with God's gracious initiative in our lives, and not striving to achieve it on our own.

We only move towards goals if we think that they are reachable. Thomas Aquinas discusses the question of how and why we remain hopeful in the Christian life, rather than becoming despairing and hopeless. He observes that when we believe there is happiness or a good that is impossible to attain, we will not even try to attempt it. We do not move towards the impossible. Once we believe that something is out of our grasp, we will cease to attempt to reach it; hopelessness sets in and we find that we can no longer summon the effort to move towards the goal. Conversely, the proper object of hope is that something is *possible* (ST II.II.20.4). When we really want something and we believe that it is achievable, we are spurred on towards the goal, even if it at times it appears challenging and difficult. This is why it is so important that we constantly stress the truth that we are changed because it is God's will; his desire and his purpose is to change us into the likeness of the Son. It is pure gift. To be sure, we must respond to his loving call, but the achievement is his and not ours, and we only respond well when we remember that we are responding to *his* gracious desire and ability to change us rather than having to change ourselves. So much of the effectiveness of our discipleship begins in our thinking. The process of becoming an apprentice is rooted in our perceptions of the character of God, the way he relates to us, his work in our lives and in the lives of those around us. So much of our discipleship is ineffective because something in our thinking has gone awry. Fundamentally, we have lost sight of the goal of the Christian life and how this goal might be achieved.

DISCIPLESHIP AS MISSION

It is easy to begin to think that discipleship is about some sort of personal quest for holiness, but that would be to put the emphasis in entirely the wrong place. The other question that is high on the agenda for the church in the West is mission. In cultures, such as Europe or Australasia (and North America is showing signs of the same trend), where the church has become increasingly marginalized and has been losing numbers overall, Christians are wondering how to reach those around them with the good news of Jesus Christ. What will be meaningful? What will be relevant? How can we make an impact on the society around us? The question of discipleship is intimately bound up with mission. There can be no effective mission without effective discipleship and vice versa. One does not follow another, but the two are mutually coinherent—they are always woven together. When we become apprentices of Jesus Christ, and learn from him, we will naturally make disciples of others. The point about learning from Jesus, loving and obeying him, is that we do so for the sake of others, in order that we are able to be ambassadors for him in the places where we live and work. The primary mark of the followers of Jesus is that they love one another in the way that Jesus has loved them (John 13:34). It is impossible, therefore, for discipleship to be an individual pursuit, and it is impossible to become an apprentice of Jesus without learning to love those around us. A community of apprentices who has learned about this love, and learned how to put it into practice with one another, will have a powerful witness to the world.

BECOMING FOLLOWERS OF JESUS

Jesus taught that to follow him is perfect freedom. Discipleship is about freedom: freedom to love God with our whole hearts and freedom to love one another without the distortions of lies, manipulation, hatred, and lust. Becoming an apprentice of Jesus means freedom from shame, freedom to follow the Spirit wherever he takes us, freedom from worry, freedom from materialism and greed, and freedom from the weight of despair and hope-lessness. This life of freedom was lived and modeled by Jesus. He lived a human life, and died a human death, not only to free us from the slavery of sin, but in doing that, to begin to transform our lives to look like his. This is at the heart of the gospel, and therefore, should be at the heart of discipleship. The heart of the gospel is not just an assent to a proposition or a signing up to a creed. Of course, that is the perfect beginning. "I believe . . ." is the first step, the first "yes" to Christ, and it is for this reason we desire to witness that "yes" in others. Evangelists have a gift of bringing people to that moment of assent to Christ. Many of us, however, do not begin our life of discipleship here. We come to Jesus for countless reasons, but having encountered him, the realization that he is the Savior, *our* Savior, changes the way we follow him. Jesus Christ is the only one who opens the way for us to the Father, the only one who gave up his life for us so that we could be free. When we know the truth of this, our lives are filled with gratitude and praise to God. Apprentices are worshippers and followers. Some worship and then follow, others follow first, and then come to worship.

The first disciples were called to follow Jesus before they worshipped him. They knew him first as a teacher and a Rabbi—a man of wisdom and authority. Not only this, but his teaching was accompanied by acts of power that astonished those around him. Following Jesus was not a boring life of rules and regulations. In fact, Jesus was remarkably free from rules and regulations, which made his life so offensive to the rule-bound Pharisees. For the disciples, it was the most thrilling, challenging, powerful, horrifying, and wonderful adventure they had ever faced. What does it mean for us to "follow" Jesus? I sometimes think that many people imagine following Jesus to be like the way a tired child trails after her parents on a long and boring walk. We do it because we have to, or because it is "good for us," but quite frankly, it is not much fun. For others, following Jesus has become about following rules, or playing a role, but our hearts are not in it. I see following Jesus as having many different aspects to it. Sometimes it is like following a dance partner. If we are learning how to dance, we will learn much more quickly if we are teamed up with an expert. He or she will guide us, steer us, and make us ten times the dancer we might have been if we had been teamed up with a less experienced person. Learning to dance is a mixture of hard work, challenge, and fun at the same time. It can feel awkward when we get it wrong and liberating when we get it right. We can be amazed at what we can learn, and gratified when something we have worked at for hours becomes second nature. Learning any new skill can be like this, but dancing with a partner is a picture of the dynamic of learning closely from someone else, and following their every move. When we become Christians, it should feel as if we have been teamed up with the best partner ever—the one who truly knows how to live life well, who will patiently teach us the steps, and whose partnership will make us more than we are in our own strength. He will teach us, not as one who shouts instructions through a megaphone, tutting frustratedly when we mess up, but as one who dances with us, guiding, steering, keeping us from slipping and falling, and when we do slip and fall, who picks us up and starts again. In some ways, following Jesus is like this.

At the risk of being prosaic, it is also like following as in "following a fitness regime" or "following a recipe." Jesus enjoined his disciples over and over again to be men and women who "put his words into practice." His teachings are the key to the good life, the free life, the life that will not be shaken. His teachings are true and they bring freedom and wholeness, wisdom and clarity. Putting his words into practice is how we learn to love God and to love one another. If we say we want to get fit, learn a language, or make a cake, and yet we refuse to follow the fitness regime, learn the vocabulary, follow the recipe, our claims to want to learn become nonsensical.

We are saying one thing with our lips, and another with our actions. Being an effective disciple begins with the humility and the desire to learn. Jesus is the Teacher and we are his pupils. Jesus is the Mentor and we are the learners. Jesus is the Master and we are his apprentices. Jesus is the Expert and we are the novices. The amazing and wonderful thing is that in order to teach us, Jesus put himself in the position of the Servant. He is the humble and gentle one, whose leading is sacrificial, and whose greatest act of power in this world was made manifest in the weakness of the cross. His leading and teaching is the opposite of authoritarian and aggressive. It is humble, and gracious and non-coercive. Jesus is the trustworthy teacher, whose teaching exists to transform our inner beings, to makes us into people we cannot imagine we could become.

APPRENTICES TO DIFFERENT ARTISANS

Tempting as it might be for us to imagine, we need to resist the idea that there is a perfect "model" or "program" of discipleship. Effective discipleship is not built on specific practices, which look the same for all people in all places. Instead, it is built on principles and values rooted in the character of God. We will probably find that we gravitate towards one picture of discipleship and one particular way of living the Christian life more than another. It may be we are captivated by those who devote their lives to the poor, or those who minister in great power, or those who work for justice for the oppressed and marginalized. Sometimes we feel more secure if we are presented with just one answer to the question of what it *really* means to be like Jesus. Similarly, we may also prefer to have "rules." If we are the sort of person who likes structures, we may prefer to be in a setting when someone in authority says, "Do this" or "Do that" and we just have to do it. Many Christian churches function in this way, but this is a concession to our human frailty rather than a good model for discipleship.

We need to recognize that becoming like Jesus in this life, will actually not be lived out in the exactly the same way in every life. God loves *diversity* and he loves *freedom*. We only have to look at creation to know that this is true. Becoming like the Son is not a call to uniformity, but a celebration of diversity, and this is a work of the Spirit. Nick and I have always encouraged those in our churches to grow in discipleship, but we try to communicate to them that there is not one particular way of doing this. We will all become apprentices to different artisans—some to those skilled in teaching and preaching, some to evangelists, some to servants of the poor, some to healers, etc. Some of us, throughout our lives, will move from one artisan to another in order to keep learning a new craft. This is good and healthy. Tom Smail writes:

> The creator Spirit brings forth a new likeness of Jesus. There are no stereotypes of sanctity. All the saints are gloriously various, but out of all the differing colours and textures of their created natures and personalities the Spirit sets himself to paint a new ikon of the Lord. Being thus in process of being recreated by the Spirit, saints begin to be themselves recreative in the communities and societies to which they belong.[1]

In becoming more like Jesus, we become more like our true selves, the persons we were created to be. One person who is formed in the likeness of the Son, will still look different from everyone else, and no one person will embody all his characteristics and gifts in this life. As a body, we will reflect more of Christ to the world than we are able to on our own. In conforming to the likeness of the Son, the uniqueness of our personhood shines ever more intensely and brightly. This is the glory of God at work in us and in the church.

THE GIFTS OF GOD TO FORM CHRIST IN US

If we first need to establish the theological principles of discipleship before we can speak about the practices, we need to recognize the means by which God forms us in the image of Christ. God has given us gifts in order to help achieve his goal in us. In chapters 3–6, we will explore each of these gifts: the gift of the Son himself, the Word of God; the gift of his Spirit, the power of God within; the gift of the lives we live, the circumstances in which we find ourselves; and the gift of one another. In all these God works to establish what has been predestined, so that we should be conformed to the likeness of the Son. In chapter 7, I offer some insights from my experience of mentoring others. The first question that must be addressed, however, as one of the key questions of discipleship, is "How much effort is required?"

1. Smail, *The Giving Gift*, 180.

two

God's Initiative and Our Response

HOW MUCH "EFFORT" IS REQUIRED?

ONE OF THE FUNDAMENTAL questions in the Christian life is "How much *effort* are we required to put in, in order to achieve the goal of becoming like Christ?" What is the part that we have to play? The pursuit of holiness is often understood in terms of spiritual "discipline," or as engaging in the spiritual disciplines. Being disciplined about a task communicates concepts like work, commitment, and effort, and the idea of effort is often expressed in the New Testament in relation to living the Christian life. We are expected to make every effort to love God and to love our neighbour as ourselves—and, in truth, this really does often feel like an effort! Jesus says that we should make every effort to enter the narrow door of the kingdom (Luke 13:24). Paul tells the Ephesians to make every effort to keep the unity of the Spirit through the bond of peace (Eph 4:3). The writer of Hebrews writes that we should make every effort to live in peace with all people and to be holy (Heb 12:14). Peter says that we should make every effort to add to our faith qualities such as goodness, knowledge, self-control, perseverance, godliness, brotherly kindness, and love (2 Pet 1:5–7). Clearly, there is something that we are responsible for, something that we can do to live life well as God intends for us. But where does this effort come from and what does it achieve in us?

Our part in living a God-filled life is only ever in response to what God has already done for us and in us. The effort that we make is our response to God's great gifts poured out into our lives. Paul begins his letter to the Ephesians with an overflow of praise to God for his abundant blessings. God, in his mercy, has not only chosen us, but has chosen us to become holy and blameless. When Paul talks about what has been "predestined," it is not with reference to those who might have been eternally chosen, and those who might have been eternally damned. Paul refers to the truth that those whom God has chosen will be adopted as sons and daughters, and will be conformed to his likeness. What has been predestined, decided beforehand, is that followers of Jesus will eventually look like him. "For those God foreknew he also predestined *to be conformed to the likeness of his Son*, that he might be the firstborn among many brothers" (Rom 8:29. See also Eph 1:1–5). This is the work of the Spirit in the life of a believer. That is God's will for humanity, and it is through God's great gift to us, of his Son and his Spirit, that he will accomplish this in us. God gives freely, lavishly, and unconditionally in order to bring this about in our lives. Peter writes, "His divine power *has given us everything we need* for life and godliness through our knowledge of him who called us by his own glory and goodness" (2 Pet 1:3). We are hidden in Christ. As he is in us, and we are in him, so Christ's own righteousness and his holiness become ours.

Clearly, on the one hand then, this process of becoming like Jesus, is purely and simply in *God's* hands. He is faithful and he will do it. On the other hand, however, we have some part to play in the transformation of our lives. We are encouraged to make every effort to behave well—towards God and towards others. How are we to understand this dynamic? If it is all God's work in us, and God has chosen this for us beforehand, why do we need to make any effort at all, and what should that effort look like?

ENGAGING WITH GOD, WITH ONE ANOTHER, AND WITH THE WORLD

When human beings are extremely passive, they fail to thrive and flourish. Extreme passivity restricts development and growth, and when people live in conditions where they are subjected to total powerlessness, it is the very resourceful and the resistant who succeed in rising above the crushing and dehumanizing nature of those conditions. God's purpose for humanity is that we govern and steward well within our sphere of influence. Human beings are created to take responsibility for the environment in which they live and operate. This is true whether it is a parent in a family, a teacher in a classroom, a CEO of a company, or a president of a country. We all have a sphere of influence, whether great or small. Moreover, whether or not we have positions of responsibility, we all have a responsibility to those around us, and this extends not just to people, but to our environment as well, to the physical place in which we live. Willard speaks about this sphere of influence as a "kingdom"—a kingdom being the "range of our effective will." We all affect the world around us, whether for good or ill, because we have been created to exercise our own wills: to make choices, to voice opinions, and to have an impact on our surroundings. It is within our power to create conditions for others and, literally, for the creation, where there is health and life, just as it is within our power to neglect and destroy. This is true in relation to all the people who are part of our lives just as it is true of gardens, buildings, cities, parks, farms, etc. Human beings have the ability to nurture, tend, feed, and encourage, just as they have the ability to neglect, abuse, and destroy.

At the very heart of the Christian faith is a message about what it means to flourish as a human being, and in this flourishing, to become an agent of transformation in the world. Jesus lived a human life on this earth that was a life fully alive, and his promise to those who follow him is that this life is for them too. When God became man in Christ, he brought about three dynamic changes for humanity. First, by living, dying, and being raised to life in his humanity, he defeated the power of sin and death. All the destructive and deathly forces in this world are disempowered in Jesus's life, death, and resurrection. Secondly, he modeled a life that is the perfect human life, full of the power and the Spirit of God. And thirdly, he gave us the means to live that life as well. By becoming like us, he made it possible for us to become like him. The good news of the coming of God's kingdom is that when we place our trust in Jesus Christ, the fullness of human life is available for us, in him. However, in order to live the fully human life that God intends for us, we have to learn to engage with this kingdom life. We have to learn how to engage with God and with one another in ways that are both sacrificially loving and entirely truthful. Engaging in the life of God's kingdom brings us freedom and empowerment, and is what a fully human life should look like. The means of engaging in the kingdom life is to learn to put our trust in Jesus Christ, and the effort that is required of us in the Christian life can be summed up in this phrase: "to trust in Jesus Christ."

FAITH AND TRUST

Faith in God is a gift from him. We cannot make ourselves believe in the truth and reality of God. We believe in him because he reveals himself to us and, by his Spirit, opens our eyes to the truth. The word that we use for "faith" however, does not just mean to believe, but also *to trust*. Faith and trust are very closely linked, but we use them in slightly different ways. Having faith that Jesus is the Son of God and that he died "for me" so that I could live a new life is a first step in the Christian life, but it does not sum up the whole of the Christian life. Living our whole lives in an active and dynamic relationship with God requires us to learn how to trust him. We have to learn how to trust God in a multitude of ways and in every circumstance. This is something that we have to learn over time, mainly because we can never predict what will happen next. We can learn to trust him in one particular circumstance, but then we find ourselves in a different situation, where we have to trust God for something else in a completely new way. God leads us through every circumstance teaching us his trustworthy ways. Learning to trust God means we will learn he is who he says he is, his ways are best in every circumstance, his promises are true, he works all things for good for those who love him, and nothing is impossible for him. Learning these new ways of thinking and behaving requires an effort from us, because they are not the ways of the world. We need a new mindset. It is, in fact, a new way of perceiving reality, which will then change the way we operate. Paul talks about this as having the "mind of Christ." Faith and trust are not passive, but active, as we will go on to see. In the next few chapters, we will explore what we might be able to do to respond to the work of God in us: how we might grow in childlike trust and obedience to the living God.

JESUS AS OUR MODEL?

We are used to hearing that Jesus himself is our model for discipleship, and as we have seen, the imitation of Christ, and of others, is a part of discipleship, but in what way do we mean this? When Jesus lived on this earth it was as a particular person in a particular culture. He was a first century Palestinian Jewish man. He engaged with people in his own culture, in his own time, and as only he, as this particular man, could. Our lives are nothing like his in terms of our own culture and personhood. Moreover, Jesus is perfect, and we are not. Now, the ascended Christ sits at the right hand of the Father, the entire universe is in his hands, and he is the Savior of the world. In what way can we be "like Jesus" and imitate him? Can we really model our lives on the life of Jesus, and if so, what does that mean?

The recent "What Would Jesus Do?" movement has caught the imagination of (mostly) young people, giving rise to a whole market of WWJD bracelets, stickers, and paraphernalia. The idea behind the campaign is right. Christians should be asking themselves in different situations, "How would Jesus respond, and how might this be a guide to my own response?" The problem with the WWJD movement (and many other models of discipleship), however, is that it gives the impression that discipleship is a case of copying Jesus's actions in the things we do. This can be somewhat misleading and ultimately unhelpful. When we say that Jesus's life serves as a model for our own, what are we talking about? If we answer this question solely on the basis of what Jesus does, the interesting thing is, that we come up with a whole number of different answers depending on whom we ask. Some Christians are concerned solely with justice issues and serving the poor. They have devoted their lives to this end. If we ask them, "What Would Jesus Do?" the answer would be simple. He gave his life to the poor, and so should we. Others would say that Jesus was a revolutionary figure, overturning the religious establishment of his day, and challenging the status quo. What Would Jesus Do? Challenge the institutional hierarchies and churches that exist in the world today. Still others would say that Jesus went about healing the sick, casting out demons and raising the dead. What Would Jesus Do? And so on.

Models of discipleship are often very dependent on the personalities of a particular leader, and a particular interpretation of the life of Jesus. This can be very helpful if we find that our own personalities, lifestyles, and perspectives resonate with a specific model. If we are naturally disciplined people, we will enjoy a disciplined approach. We will appreciate order and systems of learning. If we are traditional, we might find our model of discipleship within an institution. If we are anti-institutional and anti-hierarchical we will appreciate the call of the "revolutionary Jesus," and we will probably learn about discipleship in small groups away from an institutional church. If we like the boundary-breaking message of the Pentecostal movement, we will go out and offer to pray for the sick and to prophesy over people in shopping malls and on the streets. If we believe that God's heart is primarily for the poor, we will live out a life of discipleship only with the poor and the marginalized. None of these models of discipleship are "wrong." In fact, they are all right. We cannot, however, do them all, and the problem for us is that we are often presented with one model as the *only* one. If this happens to be a model that we personally cannot engage with, we are left feeling inadequate and a bit hopeless in our attempts to follow Christ. Before we begin to think about what Jesus would do, and to give our plethora of answers, there is something more fundamental that we should be focusing on when we say that Jesus's life should serve as a model for our own.

THE FATHER AND THE SON

The fully human life that is first modeled in the incarnate Jesus is the life of greatest intimacy and dependence on the Father, in the power of the Spirit. Jesus lives a human life in total love and obedience to the Father, and all that he does, he does in the power of the Spirit. Even though Jesus was God made man, he lived his life on this earth as we live ours, dependent upon the Holy Spirit for strength, encouragement, empowerment, and anointing. Throughout this book, we will come back again and again to Jesus's relationship with the Father in the power of the Spirit, as our central theme of discipleship. It seems a strange thing to say that Jesus exercised faith in God on this earth—after all, he is God! When he took on a human nature, however, he submitted his fully divine life to being lived out in a human way. He was constrained and constricted by a bodily existence. He felt pain, hunger, thirst, and tiredness. He experienced loneliness, frustration with his friends, longings, and temptations. In all of these experiences, he related to his Father *through the Holy Spirit*. It was in the power of the Spirit that he lived a life of unwavering trust in the Father, even to the point of giving up his life. His life of faith and obedience was the first perfect life ever lived, and in this, it was also the perfection of faith and obedience. It is his life of faith that is, first and foremost, the template for our lives. Jesus is both the author and perfecter of our faith. He trod the path of the life of faith first, he imparts this faith to us, and he perfects it in us. It is this life of unwavering trust that is perfect freedom and is a life fully lived.

The story of the Bible is the story of God's covenant relationship with humanity. The covenant began with Abraham, was inherited by the Jewish people, his descendants, and then, through Christ, was extended to all who believe in him. God's covenant promise to the descendants of Abraham was one of belonging, "I will be your God and you will be my people." This promise is then extended through his Son to those who put their faith in him, and this promise that God has made to us cannot be broken. It is unconditional. It is his promise to us. It is possible, however, to live this life as though God's promise is untrue or meaningless. Jesus came to earth to establish this covenant relationship in a new way. The promises of God remain, that he will be our God and we will be his people. The way we learn about this promise, however, is now through Jesus Christ, and the way we participate in this relationship is through him and in the grace of the Spirit. The new covenant is not just the re-establishing of the relationship of God with humanity, but the revelation that God, who created the heavens and the earth, is also our Father and our perfect parent. Jesus's life on earth embodies the promises of the covenant, and the way in which he lived demonstrates the dynamic of life in the kingdom. This is all rooted in his relationship with the Father in the power of the Spirit. As we live with God, we learn more and more about the truths of the covenant: that he is unswervingly and endlessly faithful to us, and that he truly will never leave us or forsake us. As we learn about the God of the covenant in Christ and the Spirit, we learn to respond to him with lives that are full of love, trust, and obedience. This is what Jesus has modeled first for us.

So, life in a covenant relationship with God is not passive. Jesus himself was not passive in his relationship with the Father. He was submissive and yielding to the purposes of the Father, but he was active in his response. A life of faith and trust requires a response from us. The purpose of God for human beings is that we participate in the life of the kingdom of God and that we take an active role in that. His kingdom will come in spite of us, but in his mercy, he has chosen to allow us to work with him—not for his sake, but for ours—for the good of the world. It is in participating in the life of the kingdom that we learn the ways and the character of God and co-operating with God is the key dynamic of discipleship—it underpins the whole Christian life. The gifts of faith and trust are given so that we are able to follow, and following Jesus is an active pursuit that affects our whole lives.

FOLLOWING FREELY

One of the first things that Jesus did in his public ministry was to gather followers, and what he taught them were the ways of faith. The stories we have of the calling of the disciples, Peter and Andrew, James and John, Matthew and Nathaniel, are relatively brief. It really does appear that they left everything at once and followed him. This picture of the immediate obedience of his first disciples can sometimes be a bit intimidating for us, especially when it appears that Jesus rebukes those who might procrastinate, make excuses, or find something better to do (Luke 9:57–62)! Jesus has uncompromising words for those who follow him. No one who puts their hand to the plough and looks back is fit for service in the kingdom of God. There is a cost to discipleship. Over the years, I have heard many preachers and teachers focus on these portrayals of discipleship, and consequently, they depict the life of discipleship in strict and uncompromising terms. Moreover, I have often heard references to the lives of great saints of the past (or sometimes the present) whose lives are made to sound remarkably perfect. It is wonderful and important to celebrate the lives of the saints, and to have spiritual "heroes" and "heroines." It does not help us however, to portray any particular human being as nearly faultless in their Christian "walk." We would only need to ask somebody's wife, husband, sister, brother, work colleagues, or anyone who has been close to that person, to discover that he or she is probably not quite as patient, holy, compassionate, and Christlike as we might have first thought.

The problem with the uncompromising view of discipleship is that we can easily give and get the impression that discipleship is not for the hardhearted, or the faint-hearted, or the half-hearted. But the truth is that we are *all* hard-hearted, faint-hearted, and half-hearted at different times. We can *all* be proud, scared, and lazy—even mature and wonderful Christians— and sometimes we can be all three at the same time! We *all* compromise, stumble, and fail, and whereas it is right to encourage and inspire one another with tales of spiritual heroism, we must be truthful at the same time. The Bible is a brilliant example of this. We read stories of great men and women of faith who are honored by God, and by the people of God. People like Abraham, David, Rahab, and Deborah are the faithful who, at the same time, were also fearful, proud, murderous, lustful, cowardly, scheming, and vain. This is a great encouragement to us. Similarly, the New Testament tells stories of people who followed Jesus, but who did not always get it right. The disciples may have left everything to follow Jesus straight away, but in their following, they were sometimes scared, sometimes lazy, sometimes proud, and sometimes blind to what God was doing in their midst. Even after Pentecost, the stories in Acts are certainly not of a perfect church, and reading Paul's letters gives us an insight into the conflict, chaos, and confusion that was reigning in the young churches he had established.

We can begin to follow Jesus for a whole number of reasons. It becomes clear throughout the Gospel stories that the first disciples did not know at once that he was the Messiah. Their understanding developed over time. They grew in their faith. Maybe they had heard his teaching and were astonished by it. Maybe he had healed one of their family members. Maybe, like Nathaniel, he spoke into their lives in a way that amazed them. They were clearly captivated by him, but they did not fully understand who he was. Our understanding of God grows over a lifetime. We understand in stages, as the Spirit works in our hearts and our minds, revealing truths about God to us, breaking down our reserve, our pride, our stubbornness, and our fear. Following Jesus will entail many highs and lows. We will have times of great intimacy with God, times of great revelation and peace, and times when we make colossal mistakes and when we are wracked with guilt and remorse. We might have times when we feel bored or disconnected in our church family, and other times when we feel that the same Christian community is showing us a glimpse of heaven.

Faith and trust sometimes means witnessing amazing and wonderful answers to prayer and sometimes means just hanging in there and refusing to follow anyone else. The disciples, and the early church, were taken on a rollercoaster ride of witnessing the extraordinary power of Jesus on the one hand, and devastating weakness on the other. In Luke 10, Jesus appoints seventy-two disciples and sends them out on a mission to preach, to demonstrate the good news of the kingdom, to do what he has been doing. They come back thrilled and excited by what they have witnessed, "Lord, even the demons submit to us in your name." The feeling of power and energy must have been exhilarating. Even Jesus is full of joy at what they have seen and done. It is a moment of intense joy for all involved—a spiritual high. In contrast, in John 6 we read of a completely different dynamic between Jesus and his followers. Jesus begins to teach his followers about his death, but in graphic and distasteful terms. Not only will his followers have to participate in his death, but in order to do this, they will have to eat his flesh and drink his blood. Only this will be the way to eternal life. Not surprisingly, at this point, many disciples desert him, and those who are left, grumble! What a different picture of discipleship from Luke 10. When Jesus asks them if they will leave too, Peter replies, "Lord to whom shall we go? You have the words of eternal life, and we have believed, and have come to know that you are the Holy One of God."

Following Jesus is not a simple, straightforward path onwards and upwards. It entails setbacks and disappointments as well as times of extraordinary delight. The only constancy comes from God. This is because he allows us to follow freely, but in following freely, we learn how to live lives that are truly free. Throughout our lives, we are not coerced but wooed by Jesus, like a lover woos a somewhat reluctant beloved. He waits patiently for us; he wins our hearts; he allays our fears; he shows us where we are making mistakes; he is gentle with us when we are selfish, mean-spirited, spiteful, unforgiving. He does not treat us as our sins deserve, but forgives us and goes on forgiving us, so that we can live lives that are full and free. I love the end of one of the sections of *The Didache*, an early Christian catechism, where the writer says, "If you can shoulder the Lord's yoke in its entirety, then you will be perfect; but if that is too much for you, do as much as you can" (§6). I do not understand this as a defeatist philosophy. It does not mean, do what you can and give up on the things you cannot do, but it means keep your focus on that which you *can* do. My experience of watching and learning from others in the life of discipleship is that those who keep doing as much as they can are the ones who, over time, keep learning to do more and more, and go from strength to strength.

DISCIPLESHIP FOR MEN, WOMEN, AND CHILDREN

Most of the stories we read in the Gospels focus on the twelve disciples who, of course, were all men. Moreover, discipleship is often equated with leadership, and the worldwide church has more men than women in official positions of "leadership." Jesus, however, had men and women among his followers, and it is important in our teaching on discipleship that we do not subconsciously exclude women. The Gospels make it clear that Jesus was radical in his choosing and inclusion of women among his close group of disciples. Kenneth Bailey, in his book, *Jesus through Middle Eastern Eyes*, makes the point that Jesus, in his treatment of women, made a decisive break with the traditional cultural separation of men and women. In Matthew 12, when Jesus is told that his mother and his brothers are outside waiting for him, he responds by stretching out his hand toward his disciples, and saying, "Here are my mother and my brothers! For whoever does the will of my Father in heaven is my brother, and sister, and mother." Jesus would only have referred to the women in this way if they had been there with him. Bailey makes the point that the disciples in that room with Jesus were men *and* women.[1]

1. Bailey, *Jesus through Middle Eastern Eyes*, 192.

Similarly, Luke reports that a number of women not only traveled with Jesus but also funded his mission. For women to travel with a rabbi as his followers was revolutionary in that time (Luke 8:1–3). Luke also tells the story of Mary and Martha, Mary who sat at Jesus's feet and listened to his teaching, and her sister Martha, who was distracted and worried by many things (Luke 10:38). To sit at a person's feet and listen to their teaching was the phrase used of a disciple with a rabbi. Mary was Jesus's disciple, sitting with the men, and listening to him.[2] Moreover, in Acts 9:36, the feminine form of the word disciple, *mathetria*, is used of Tabitha (Dorcas). The Bible does not tell stories of specific children following Jesus; however, contrary to most artistic representations of the disciples as middle-aged men, we know that some of the disciples were very young men. They could have been anywhere from the mid-to-late teenage years. When we understand that the life of discipleship is about nurturing the life of faith and trust, we see at once how this is open to all, and why Jesus drew a young child into his arms to illustrate the point that unless we become like children, we have not yet learned the secret of the kingdom of God. Children are naturally trusting of those who care for them, and only when adults prove themselves to be untrustworthy does a child become wary and cynical. The life of trusting and following Jesus is open to all—men, women, and children.

FINDING A TREASURE OF INFINITE WORTH

Following freely is one of the keys to following joyfully, and following joyfully allows us to follow freely. The two are interconnected. Recently, one of my grown-up sons was facing a tiresome but necessary task. It had to be done, and we had talked quite a bit about the fact that he just had to knuckle down and do it and how he might go about it. He knew that I had very definite ideas about what that should look like, so when he came to me one day and told me that he knew it had to be done, but that he was not going to do anything about it for a while longer, he was fully expecting me to give him a lecture, and to put pressure on him to do it straight away. Despite very much wanting him to get on with it, I knew he was tired and fed up, and I also realized that actually, he was grown up now and if he wanted to procrastinate, then that was up to him. I told him that really it was fine by me, and if he wanted to wait a bit longer, it was totally up to him. He promptly went off and did what he needed to do! There is something about

---

2. Ibid., 192–93.

knowing we are free to choose and free to follow that helps us to follow joyfully. Most of us do not like being "told what to do," and if we do what we do simply out of a sense of fear or duty, there will come a time when we rebel. Jesus never forced anyone to "do what they were told." Willard writes, "the Christian stands, not under the dictatorship of a legalistic 'You ought,' but in the magnetic field of Christian freedom, under the empowering of the 'You may.'"[3] If we live under the legalistic "you ought," we will either never get started on the life of following Jesus, or we will soon run out of energy. Something else will come along that will appear easier, more fun, and far more attractive. The only way we can possibly persevere in the life of following Jesus is if we are wholly convinced, like Peter, that there is no one and nothing else worth following, and if this conviction comes from our hearts. Jesus himself described this as finding a treasure of infinite worth, a pearl of great price. It is a tragedy that there are people both inside and outside the church who cannot understand that the Christian life is the greatest gift ever, and the ultimate way of freedom.

Jesus, after all, for all his hard sayings, taught that following him was the greatest freedom and greatest joy a human being could ever experience. Moreover, he teaches that to learn from him leads to rest and peace for our souls. The reason that we want to take his yoke upon us is because it brings peace and joy. The opposite of the freedom and the joy Jesus describes is legalism—adhering to a set of rules for the sake of the rules. Legalism is rigid and inflexible, and leads us to imagine that we are only accepted on the basis of whether we do the "right" thing or not. It is the opposite of grace (the idea that God accepts us regardless of what we have done). Legalism can sometimes feel safe, because we are told what to do and how to behave, but it fails to allow us to grow up and to mature, and in the end it becomes oppressive and wearisome. Jesus berates the Pharisees and the teachers of the law because they create burdens that are too heavy for people to carry. "And you experts in the law, woe to you, because you load people down with burdens they can hardly carry, and you yourselves will not lift one finger to help them" (Luke 11:46).

I have been surprised, over the years, to see how many people seem to be happier in a more highly controlled environment, where they are given definite answers, and where they are told what to do and how to behave. In some churches, church members are expected to (literally) sign to a particular creed and particular doctrines, and those who cannot sign to those

3. Willard, *The Great Omission*, 12.

doctrines are not accepted. I have also heard of churches where the pastors dictate what lifestyle choices the members of their congregations should make, whom they should date and marry, where they should live, where their children should go to school, etc. Of course, there are degrees of control, and this ranges from the worst form, which is a cult, to the more subtle forms that exist in many institutions. Moreover, there are certain environments where those responsible for maintaining order must exercise some control, otherwise things would descend into anarchy. No one who works in a school would wish to relinquish certain aspects of control! Control is necessary when there is a threat to an individual or to the community, and this is only right and proper. There certainly may be times when an individual or a group becomes a destructive influence within a community, either through their teaching or their actions, in which case, some form of exclusion might be necessary. A church, however, in its local expression, is a voluntary organization and, dangerous elements apart, should function in a different way. In a church, or Christian group, any degree of control is potentially open to abuse. It may be necessary at times to safeguard a fellowship from disruptive influences, but no congregation will develop mature and Christlike relationships if they are controlled. This is why, in a church setting, it is so important that one human being or a group of human beings cannot and must not dictate what other people think and do. Unless someone is a direct threat to the safety of others (by which I also mean emotional safety), people should not be controlled, but respected and listened to. If we have a disagreement, we do not coerce one another, but we request and persuade. Paul's letters are a wonderful example of this. We will come back to this theme in a later chapter.

We are not forced, therefore, into behaving in a certain way. On the other hand, Jesus is clear that those who love him *will* obey him. In John's Gospel, Jesus talks to his disciples about the joy, freedom, and fullness of life that is promised to those who follow him, and who live life in relationship with the Father, as he himself lives. Loving Jesus is completely bound up with living in him, and through him, living in the Father, and then through this, being enabled to keep his commandments. And this is total freedom. Seeing the world as Jesus sees the world sets us free. "As the Father has loved me, so have I loved you. Abide in my love. If you keep my commandments, you will abide in my love, just as I have kept my Father's commandments and abide in his love. These things I have spoken to you, that my joy may be in you, and that your joy may be full" (John 15:9–11). Jesus promises not just joy, but life, and a life that will go on forever.

It might seem strange to say I feel something is missing from the Bible, but when I read the stories of Jesus and his followers, I sometimes wish the Gospel writers would have told us how they laughed together. I feel sure that Jesus made his followers laugh, and they him. I do not believe the joy they shared together was just manifested in a pious glow, but instead in hearty and unrestrained laughter. I love being with people who make me laugh, and one of the things I have noticed over and over again is that when a group of people have been together praying and worshipping and sharing stories of God's goodness, the time so often ends in laughing together. Laughter achieves so many things. It is not only healing for our souls, but it binds us together, relieves tense situations, and helps us to cope with tragedy and pain. It is a gift from God, and in my experience, encounters with Jesus release laughter.

LIVING FOREVER

Jesus prays for his disciples, "Father, the hour has come; glorify your Son that the Son may glorify you, since you have given him authority over all flesh, to give eternal life to all whom you have given him. And this is eternal life, that they know you the only true God, and Jesus Christ whom you have sent" (John 17:1–3). When my family and I lived in Zimbabwe, we were confronted with much more death than we are in England. In Zimbabwe and, of course, in so many countries in the world, many more people die young, infant mortality rates are higher, and more accidents and untreated sicknesses lead to death. People are no less devastated by loss when they are used to death, but they are more accepting that it is a part of life. When we moved back to England, we noticed a huge difference in how all people, including Christians, dealt with death. In Zimbabwe, Christians talk of heaven more. The hope of heaven is real, and we lived with a strong awareness that this life was not the only life there is. I have been largely sheltered from untimely deaths in my own family, but in Zimbabwe, we lived closely with those who suffered real tragedies. One of the spiritual truths that this opened up to me was that this life on earth really is not the only life. This does not mean, however, that we just get this life over and done with so that we can get to heaven and really start living, but that this life is the beginning of the eternal one to come. For this reason, what we do here matters. Our lives here have eternal significance. And in this process of transformation, we are in the process of becoming the people we will be forever.

The relationship of this life to the next is not that one ends and then the next one begins. It is not as if everything here will be obliterated, and God will start all over again. God's plan for his creation is that it will be re-created and renewed. A renewal is different from a ripping up and starting again; it is the process of taking what is there already and reshaping and reforming it. The pot the potter is fashioning is a work in progress. The clay does not get thrown out and a new lump chosen for a better pot, but the clay under his hands is constantly being coaxed into shape, even if that takes a long time. The stuff we are made of now will somehow always be the stuff we are made of, but it will be shaped and formed into perfection by the two hands of God, the Son and the Spirit. So what we do with our lives here and now matters because we are going to have an eternal existence. The question we need to face is, would we live our lives differently now if we were more aware of the fact that the good we are capable of doing now will cause ripples into eternity? Dallas Willard writes, "We are, all of us, never-ceasing spiritual beings with a unique eternal calling to count for good in God's great universe."[4] Would we change the way we live now if we realized that we, and the people around us, are never going to stop living?

Jesus talks about storing up treasure in heaven for ourselves. What does this mean? He speaks of treasures in heaven in contrast to the material treasures of earth, which will not last. Material things are not bad in them-selves, just by virtue of being "things." They become damaging when we need them to feed, either our insecurities, our envy, our greed, or all three. If I want "things"—money, cars, houses, gadgets, clothes, certificates—in order to give me a sense of identity, or to feed certain longings, or simply just to have what everyone else has, then the things will stand in the way of storing up treasures in heaven. They will stand in the way because I will not be prepared to let them go, because I cannot "afford" to. Then the hold-ing on to them will prevent me from growing into freedom. I will cease to be able to be free and generous when it comes to possessions because I have invested so much of my "self" in them. God's will for our lives is that our identities are formed, first and foremost, as those who are "in Christ." Material things will not last forever, but our beings, our very selves, and the relationships that we form, will.

There was a young woman in one of our churches who became a Christian during our Alpha course, and soon after this, she had a re-markable incident. After becoming a Christian, she got into the practice

4. Willard, *The Divine Conspiracy*, 29.

of reading daily Bible notes, and one Saturday she read Matthew 6:19–24 (Jesus's teaching on treasure in heaven). After reading it, she commented to her grandmother just what good and sensible advice it was. The next day, when she was in church on Sunday, her house was burgled and all the electronic goods were taken. A few days after that she read Heb 12:5ff., and was struck by verse 11: "No discipline seems pleasant at the time, but painful. Later on, however, it produces a harvest of righteousness and peace for those who have been trained by it." As a result of her Bible readings, and the burglary, she made a decision not to replace the electronic goods for a while until she had learned to live more simply, and so as not to have endless distractions at home. She is now an ordained minister. She wrote this to me recently about the incident, "I think it was significant for me at the time as I was learning to be attentive to God through Scripture—or actually rather, I was learning that God was attentive to me through Scripture—even more amazing!"

OUR RESPONSE

We cannot, by our own effort, develop the character of Christ in us. We cannot possibly make ourselves like God. However, we also are not made to be simply passive in the Christian life. This would be to forfeit some of the fullness of life in the kingdom of God. If God has given us everything we need to participate in the divine nature, and to become Christlike, how do we respond? How do we *add* to our faith? There are four foundational ways in which we co-operate with the grace of God in our lives: repentance, confession, receiving and giving forgiveness, and humility. Through this we demonstrate four aspects of the Christian life that lie at the heart of transformation: love for God, love for one another, the desire to change, and the desire to learn.

We often think of repentance as being something we do at the beginning of the Christian life. Jesus came preaching a message, "Repent, for the kingdom of heaven is near." Sinners are called to repentance, to turn from godless ways, and to follow him. Repentance is a turning away from one way of living and a turning towards a new way, in which Jesus Christ is Lord. This, however, is not a one-off event, but a continual process. The process of allowing Jesus Christ to be Lord of our lives (our thoughts, speech, actions, desires, emotions, memories, relationships, and so on) is lifelong. Moreover, it is characterized by starts and stops, successes and failures, progress and setbacks. It is more like being on the dodgems than on the merry-go-round! At times we are racing round the track, neatly avoiding everything in our way, at other times we feel as if we have been hit sharply from behind. And then, of course, there are the times when we just crash. Repentance is the response of those who have first experienced God's grace. His love and compassion are so great, and his mercy is so boundless. It is because of this that we know we can turn towards him without any fear of punishment or reprisal. In fact, like the father in the story of the prodigal son, that is what God is waiting and longing for. The reality is that we often find ourselves in the far country yet again, or find that in certain areas of our lives that we still behave as if we were in the far country, and so repentance is a process, summed up by the minister who said, "I have to become a Christian every morning."

To confess something is to make it known, to speak it out. There are two types of confession in the Christian life, and both are important. One confession we make is "Jesus is Lord." We make public confessions of Jesus's Lordship, and that he is *our* Lord, in the Creed, in baptism, by taking part in communion, and, in fact, every time we admit, in public, that we are Christians. Speaking out a belief in front of others changes the way we live that belief out. Once we have owned a particular creed, there is then pressure to demonstrate that our lives bear that belief out. If we tell everyone we are committed to giving to the poor, or recycling, or hospitality, and yet there is no evidence of that in our lives, then others are entitled to question us on our confession. Is it genuine, or are we being hypocrites? Our confession of Jesus as Lord reminds us that we will then be expected to demonstrate that in some way, and thus it strengthens our obligation to live out lives that reflect his Lordship.

The other use of confession is to confess our sins, to speak out the ways in which we have fallen short of God's standards. This springs from repentance. In the Protestant churches, we often say a corporate confession, but we no longer practice the confession of our sins to a priest. In whatever form we practice it, confession of sin should be a part of our corporate life together. James links the confession of sin to healing, "Therefore, confess your sins to one another and pray for one another, that you may be healed" (Jas 5:16). John writes, "If we say we have no sin, we deceive ourselves, and the truth is not in us. If we confess our sins, he is faithful and just to forgive us our sins and to cleanse us from all unrighteousness" (1 John 1:8–9). Confession, therefore, is linked to healing and cleansing, but confession only becomes healing and cleansing when we receive forgiveness for what we have done wrong. It will not heal us to confess our sins, if we are then met with shock, anger, or disapproval from those to whom we make our confession. It is confession and forgiveness, from God and from one another, that brings healing. We will return to the value of confession one to another in a later chapter.

The receiving and giving of forgiveness is the third way in which we are called to respond to the gift of the abundant grace of God in our lives. We cannot forgive others unless and until we know we are forgiven, and Jesus teaches that once we have received the forgiveness of God, we simply must extend that forgiveness and mercy towards others. Extending forgiveness towards others for the hurt they have consciously or unconsciously caused us is a specifically Christian obligation. Jesus himself demonstrates this most powerfully on the cross, and teaches his disciples on a number of occasions of the necessity of receiving and extending forgiveness. It is one of the specific prayers that he teaches us, "Forgive us our sins, as we forgive those who sin against us." Like repentance and confession, forgiveness of others is a response to God's grace in our lives, but requires an effort from us. Forgiveness is hard work. We often feel we are losing something before we reap the benefits. Forgiveness requires a loss of pride, a loss of our defences, and a loss of the right to punish others for the hurt and the damage they have caused. Like the parable of the unmerciful servant, however, a refusal to forgive locks others, and ourselves, in prison. Forgiveness makes us channels of God's grace to others and liberates both us and them. Like repentance, forgiveness is a continual process, which is why Jesus teaches that we must learn to forgive, and forgive, and forgive—sometimes the same person for the same crime over and over again. Only this will break cycles of hatred, violence, and revenge.

The fourth characteristic that we need to grow in Christlikeness is humility, because it is only if we are humble that we believe we have something to learn. The very first disciples followed Jesus because they knew he was a rabbi, a teacher from whom they had much to learn. In John 8:31, Jesus says, "If you hold to my teaching you are truly my disciples." Astonishingly, Jesus calls us to learn from him because he himself is humble and gentle of heart. It is a remarkable thing to realize that we follow a God who calls himself humble, and we know that he *is* humble because when he came to earth in Christ, he gave up his glory to live among us so that we could learn from him. Humility, for us, is the prerequisite to learning. If we believe that we know everything already then we will not listen to others. Our pride will get in the way. Conversely, if we decide that we want to learn something new, whether this is a new skill, a language, or a sport, we find those who know how to do those things well and we learn from them. It would be ludicrous to set out to learn something new and then reject the advice and teaching of the experts. The more skilled our teacher, the quicker and better we learn. In Jesus, we have the supreme teacher and master of life. We will learn well from him when we submit ourselves to be his apprentices.

SPIRITUAL DISCIPLINES OR HOLY HABITS

Almost all models of discipleship will recommend engaging in various "spiritual disciplines." The word "discipline" unfortunately, carries connotations of punishment, and this can be misunderstood in two ways. Either we can feel that if we do something wrong, or step out of line, we might get punished, or we might have picked up the idea that in order to grow in holiness, we must undergo a punishing regime for our bodies, minds, and spirits. Is growing in Christlikeness really like joining an army boot camp? Is our view of the Christian life that it will inevitably be painful at the time, but we will emerge fitter, more robust and fit for the spiritual army? Many people over the years, appear to have allowed this idea of boot camp to dominate the pursuit of holiness. Some individuals and groups over the years of church history have even taken the idea of practicing the spiritual disciplines to a frightening and unhealthy extreme. Even if we ourselves have not come into contact with some of the more distasteful extreme practices of the church, we may well have met people who appear to be exerting a tremendous amount of effort in their practice of the spiritual disciplines, and who seem to view them as painful but necessary. Is this how it is meant to be or is there something that we might be missing if we are living like this? In our church, we have renamed the spiritual disciplines, *holy habits*, partly to avoid the connotations of the word "discipline," and partly to foster the idea that they are simply good habits within our power to cultivate, rather like remembering to say please and thank you, checking your mirrors when driving, or turning off the lights when you leave a room. A habit is something that has become second nature to us, and eventually, something we do without thinking.

Willard describes a discipline as any activity within our power that we engage in to enable us to do what we cannot do by direct effort.[5] Often people liken engaging in holy habits to practicing a musical instrument or training to play a sport. The more we practice certain things, the more a particular way of responding, behaving, or thinking will become a "natural" response for us. We do not have the power within ourselves to transform our basic habits of thought, feeling, and action so that our lives begin to look like the life of Christ. That power comes from outside ourselves and is the gift of God. Holy habits, however, are practices we *are* able to engage in that will enable us to appropriate and consolidate this transformation in us. The renewing of the mind Paul speaks of in Romans 12 is effected by the power of the Spirit in us, but it is consolidated in us by our steady refusal to engage in the thoughts, feelings, and actions of the sinful nature, and our willingness to obey Jesus's teachings. Holy habits facilitate this process in us. Willard divides holy habits into two categories: the disciplines of engagement, and the disciplines of abstinence. The disciplines of engagement are study, worship, celebration, service, prayer, fellowship, confession, and submission. The disciplines of abstinence are solitude, silence, fasting, frugality, chastity, secrecy, and sacrifice. We do not practice holy habits for the sake of the habit itself, we only ever practice a holy habit for the sake of the fruit it will bear in our characters. In the next four chapters, I discuss one of God's gifts to us to make us more like him. At the end of each chapter, I suggest which of these holy habits we can engage in to help us appropriate the particular gifts of God, and how they work to bring about a deeper and more lasting transformation in us.

God has given us his Word, his Spirit, the circumstances of life, and other people to help us to grow in maturity, life, and freedom. As we learn to respond to these gifts with repentance, confession, forgiveness, and humility, and as we engage in a variety of holy habits, we will enter more fully into the life of God's kingdom. And as we learn the ways of the kingdom, we will discover the secrets of a life that is truly free. Having laid the foundations for our "thinking" about apprenticeship, why and how we should respond, we now turn to the gift of God's Word to make us more like him.

5. Willard, *The Divine Conspiracy*, 221.

three

Formed by the Word

JESUS THE WORD MADE FLESH

IT MIGHT SOUND A bit strange, but when we talk about Jesus, we have to make it clear who we are actually talking about. We discussed earlier the idea that many models of discipleship are based on one person's or one community's perception of Jesus—how they understand who he is and what he does. It is essential that we study the Jesus of the Gospels, as it is from the biblical witness that we receive the revelation of God to us. As we do this, we will find that certain aspects of Jesus's life and ministry make more of an impression on us than others, and as we study the Gospels over years and years, new insights will come to us with every fresh reading or hearing. We absolutely must emphasize the *truly human* life of Christ. Jesus of Nazareth is a historical figure with a life we relate to, and whom we can get to discover by studying the Scriptures. The stories of Jesus capture our hearts, move us, puzzle us, and inspire us. We can "get to know" him from the Bible. On the other hand, he is not merely the perfect human being. The significance of his human life is that he is the invisible God made visible. It is Jesus the God-man who is both the inspiration and the one who empowers us for a life lived like his. In this chapter, we will explore the implications for us of this dual emphasis: Jesus Christ the Spirit-filled man who lived a life like ours, and Jesus Christ the eternal Son of God, who came to earth for our sake, suffered death, rose again, and is now at the right hand of the

Father, and who will one day come again to renew all things. Both these truths are crucial for discipleship because it is in being united with this Jesus that we will become like him.

In John's Gospel, Jesus is called the *Logos*—the Word. The word *logos*, is not really used in our culture except in relation to Jesus. It has no meaning for us apart from a theological meaning. *Logos* and its translation, Word, is now only God-language, but this was not always the case. When John used the word *logos*, he was using a word that was already known by those around him. In early Greek and Jewish writings, *logos* described an incredibly powerful and creative force in the universe. The idea of the *logos* expressed concepts such as the ordering, unifying principle of the universe, the source of all that exists, the means by which the world was created, and the principle that represents a bridge between the transcendent God and creation.[1] John's hearers would have understood the power and the wisdom enshrined in the concept of the *logos* in a way that is now lost to us. We have to work at recapturing the full meaning of the idea that Jesus is the Word made flesh, God the Son become man, but we do know that Jesus Christ is all that *logos* means, and even more that we cannot properly express.

The Word of God is God the Son. This *Logos* is the second person of the Trinity, and the *Logos* has come to dwell among us, as one of us. The Son of God was made man and lived on earth without ever ceasing to be God. That is the mystery of the incarnation. Some of the writers of the New Testament have tried to express this extraordinary truth. In Colossians 1:15–18 we read:

> He [Christ] is the image of the invisible God, the firstborn over all creation. For by him all things were created: things in heaven and on earth, visible and invisible, whether thrones or power or rulers or authorities; all things were created by him and for him. He is before all things and in him all things hold together.

In Hebrews 1:1–3 we read:

> In the past God spoke to our forefathers through the prophets at many times and in various ways, but in these last days he has spoken to us by his Son, whom he appointed heir of all things, and through whom he made the universe. The Son is the radiance of God's glory and the exact representation of his being, sustaining all things by his powerful word.

1. Ferguson and Wright, *New Dictionary*, 395–96.

If apprenticeship to Jesus is in order to become like him, what does this incarnation of God mean for us? He became like us so that we could become like him. Jesus Christ shows us what it means to be fully and truly human, but what does it mean to be shaped and formed by this powerful Word of God?

At the beginning of creation, the Spirit of God is brooding over the chaos, and God speaks to create life. In the next two chapters, we shall explore the movement of God in his Word and by his Spirit to create and to re-create life in us. God speaks, and with his voice, he brings things that do not yet exist into being. He speaks, and he brings the dead back to life. Paul writes in Romans 4:17 that God "gives life to the dead and calls things that are not as though they were." God's Word and his Spirit are given for creation and for re-creation, for birth and for resurrection. Jesus Christ has always been and always will be the one who is the life-giving, generative, and creative power on this earth. By entering into a relationship with Jesus, and living in him and he in us, we are connected to the life-giving force of the universe, through whom and by whom all living things come into being. In light of this, we should expect that living in him, and having him live in us, will inevitably change our very beings. And this transformation affects our whole being—our souls, our spirits, our minds, and our bodies. The Word of God brings life.

Without the sustaining power of the Word and the Spirit, we would cease to exist, and this is true for all living things, but the transforming power of both the Word and the Spirit begins to work in us in a new and different way when we acknowledge the Lordship of Jesus Christ. When we confess Jesus Christ is Lord, and put our faith and trust in him, we are united with him, and we begin the process of transformation into Christ-likeness. Worship of Jesus Christ, submission to him as the Lord of lords, and the name above all names, is the beginning of our renewal. How does God transform us through his Word, and how are we called to respond to this?

JESUS FULL OF GRACE AND TRUTH

John writes that the Son of God came to earth, "full of grace and truth." Jesus embodies both grace and truth, and encountering him means to encounter both the fullness of God's grace and the power of his truth. The grace of God is pure gift. Grace is God's freely given gift of love and favor to humanity even though we least deserve it. Grace is the fact that while we were *still* sinners, Christ died for us. We cannot earn God's favor, and there is nothing we can do to make us more loved. For me the idea of God's grace brings to mind besotted parents who look at the crumpled, messy face of their newborn baby who has just emerged from the birth canal and say, "She's just perfect!" Parents are delightfully blinkered in their adoration of their babies. God the Father looks on us and he sees us in the same way he sees his beloved Son, who is holy and blameless. We are his beloved children, and because of his grace, he sees us as perfect. Grace means that even though we are far from perfect, we come to perfection in God's eyes. When we are united with his Son, God looks on us and says, "He's perfect! She's perfect!" Of course we are not perfect now, but there will come a day when we will be, and God knows how he is going to bring this about, how he will call into being that which is not yet in existence. John writes:

> How great is the love the Father has lavished on us, that we should be called children of God! And that is what we are! The reason the world does not know us is that it did not know him. Dear friends, now we are children of God, and what we will be has not yet been made known. But we know that when he appears, we shall be like him, for we shall see him as he is. (1 John 3:1–3)

God's love is so great and so deep for us that he came to us, in Christ, to share our lives with us, to take upon himself the burden and the destruction of sin, evil, and death, in order that we could be set free. Jesus came to shine light into the darkness. The truth about God and the truth about ourselves is seen in him. The Son of God *is* truth, and the Son of God *speaks* truth, and his truthful being and speech releases us to be who we are created to be, free from fear, and in a loving relationship with our heavenly Father. The problem we face is that God's truthful speech about us is difficult to comprehend, and does not always appear to be "true" because we cannot yet see ourselves as he sees us. We all know that we are far from perfect, just as we know that the "saints" at Corinth were far from saintly! God's truthful speech about us is prophetic and creative. As he speaks words of truth over humanity about who we are in him, he is both speaking the truth over us and creating that truth in us. As he speaks to us about our identity as precious sons and daughters, he is calling that truth forth into being. We all know that words have the power to make us or break us. The proverb that claims sticks and stones can hurt more than words could not be more wrong. The girl who has grown up being told she is beautiful, interesting, intelligent, and kind will be formed by those words, just as the girl who grows up being told she is ugly, boring, stupid, and mean will be de-formed by those negative words. Words can either have a generative and a creative power or can be unbelievably destructive, creating misery and rejection. God's words about us, about who we are in Christ, are dynamically bringing about that truth in our lives.

In encountering the person of Christ, we are transformed by his power and his presence, because he is the creative power behind the universe. We are formed by the God who speaks to us in the Word. God speaks in many and various ways, through the Son, through the Scriptures, through the Spirit, and through the church. The voice of God brings healing, forgiveness, judgment, mercy, truth, and grace into our lives. Hebrews 4:12 speaks about the amazing power of the word of God. "The word of God is living and active. Sharper than any double-edged sword, it penetrates even to dividing soul and spirit, joints and marrow; it judges the thoughts and attitudes of the heart." Transformation happens as we respond in faith to the promises that come to us in the Word and the words of God spoken over us and as we learn not to harden our hearts but to love, to listen, and to obey.

TRUSTING IN THE PROMISE

God speaks to humanity through the Son, through the Bible, through preaching, through prophecy, and through the sacraments. Living by faith means trusting in the promises of God that come to us through his Word. Hebrews 11:1 begins, "Now faith is being sure of what we hope for and certain of what we do not see." The rest of chapter 11 is devoted to celebrating the great heroes of the faith from the Old Testament: Noah, Abraham and Sarah, Isaac, Jacob, Joseph, Moses, Rahab, so many in fact, that the writer does not have time to list them all and to tell all their stories. All these men and women had a promise from God, which they acted upon, and in doing so, demonstrated their trust in God's word and helped to fulfil God's plans and purposes for his people. It is true, though, that all of them had pretty chequered journeys when it came to being heroes of the faith! Being a hero of the faith will inevitably involve stumbling and falling many times, because following Jesus entails trusting in the certainty of promises that we certainly cannot prove, and that we very often doubt. Abraham, the father of our faith, trusted God implicitly at times, and up to a point at others. Asking his wife to pretend to be his sister in order to protect them all from possible violence was not his finest hour (Gen 12:10–20). However, being willing to hold a knife to his precious son's throat at God's command, demonstrates an almost unbelievable level of trust in God (Gen 22:1–19). Learning to trust in Jesus and his words, despite our apprehensions, is the heart of apprenticeship. Living by faith means making a decision to live as if the promises of God are totally true and trustworthy even when we feel that they might not be. This is mostly learned by trial and error.

All Christians are taken on journeys of faith because this is how we are formed in our relationship with God. We hear a promise and we are called to act upon it. Most of the promises God asks us to act upon are enshrined in Scripture. We are called to believe that whatever happens to us, God will work this for good for those who love him. We are called to believe God is unfailingly good, kind, compassionate, trustworthy, just, and wholly perfect. We are called to believe our lives, our futures, and the lives of those we love are in his hands, that he will never leave us or forsake us, and we are wholly loved. Acting upon these promises is testing, especially when our circumstances tell us a different story. The way our faith in the promises is proven and strengthened is not just in whether we can continue to say that we believe them, but whether we are prepared to act on them or not. Noah had to go ahead and build the ark. Abram had to leave Ur. Moses continued to present himself to Pharaoh time after time. Peter stepped out on to the water. Faith is about trusting in God's word to such an extent that we are prepared to act upon it, even when it feels risky, foolish, or stupid.

When we are called to act upon God's promises, therefore, we will always feel vulnerable, and we will always be subject to temptation. We will be tempted to act in ways that demonstrate that we do not really trust in God's word at all. Everyone is tempted at times to doubt God's word, to despair that he will fulfil it, or to seek to fulfill it in an easier way. Jesus was tempted in precisely these ways by Satan, in the desert, before his death, and even as he hung in excruciating pain on the cross. "Did God say . . . ?" or "If that's true, then prove it," are the words that Satan uses to sow doubt, fear, and despair—the opposite of what happens when God speaks. God's voice sows faith, assurance, life, and hope. Trusting in God's words to the point where we are willing to act on them lies at the heart of a dynamic life of discipleship. It may feel risky and difficult at times, but it is where we witness the power of the kingdom of God working in this world.

When we act upon a promise of God, and we see it fulfilled through answers to prayer, provision, transformed lives, we learn more and more about the supernatural life of the kingdom that is real in our natural world.

We see God at work around us. The incarnation, the Word become flesh, tells us God is involved in absolutely everything we do, and trusting in Jesus means witnessing that all the time. Somebody asked me recently why I thought God was real and I replied really, simply, it is because so much of the time I see him working, doing exactly what he said he would do. Learning to trust in God's promises means we see that truth more and more. We can and are inspired by other people's journeys of faith, but in fact, we have to learn that God is trustworthy for ourselves. Each person's journey of faith will look different from everyone else's. What we can be sure of is that once we have learned to trust for one thing, we will be called into trusting for another bigger thing, and so, in one sense, it never gets any easier. Faith is always only a gift from God, but we will all be stretched over our lifetimes to trust in new ways, ways that do not come so "naturally" to us. God will do this to expand our horizons, to lead us further and further into the dynamic life of his kingdom that transforms our world, and to demonstrate his unwavering faithfulness to us.

LIVING IN THE REALITY OF JESUS'S WORDS

Jesus is clear that those who hear his words and put them into practice will be people whose lives will not be shaken when the storms of life come against them. He promises that obedience to him brings not just peace, but joy and hope. In John's Gospel he also makes it clear that love for him is the only grounds for obedience. The love and obedience that Jesus describes, however, is the opposite of the burden of rules. He promises that if we love and obey, our lives will be marked by an abundance of life, joy, and freedom. This is what it means to abide in him. By abiding in him, we begin to take part in the creative life and energy that is the essence of God's being. We cannot begin to be people who learn to love and obey until we understand the nature of the kingdom we take part in, and one of the most important ways of doing this is to learn to love Scripture. It is through the Bible we have been given the revelation of God's nature, his being, the way he acts in this world and the hope we have in him. When we put our minds to understand the truths in Scripture, and when we come together with others in a commitment to helping one another to live out these truths, then the riches of God's kingdom will begin to be ours.

Good evangelical Christians are taught, from a young age, that every day they must set aside time to read the Bible and to pray—to have a "quiet time." In our Sunday School in Zimbabwe, the children were taught a song which went, "Read your Bible, pray every day . . . and you'll grow, grow, grow." The next verse carried with it the warning, "Don't read your Bible, forget to pray . . . and you'll shrink, shrink, shrink!" The idea that you could tell who was having their quiet times by whether they were getting bigger or smaller, Sunday by Sunday, used to make me laugh. The practice of setting aside time for God each day, or praying and studying the Bible is wonderful, although in reality many, many people really struggle to do this. Worse than that, they then struggle to admit it in certain circles because they feel that they will be disapproved of or looked down upon. It does not help anyone if we set up cultures in churches where people cannot be honest, and it is certainly, completely counter-productive to place burdens on people about a particular practice. If reading the Bible and praying every day is difficult for us, we must be able to admit it. On the other hand, we do not want to give up just because it is hard. The reason that through the ages Christians have urged one another to set aside time for God each day, is because it is one of the ways in which we allow God to transform us and mold us. The practices of daily worship, prayer, Bible study, and consciously placing ourselves in God's presence, all effect a multitude of changes in our lives. Volumes and volumes have been written on each of these practices on their own, on the power and the necessity of each one of them. In this chapter, I do not specifically focus on worship and prayer, but I do see them as integral to the practice of listening to God's word, and acting on it in faith, so when I speak of studying or meditating on Scripture, I mean to include worship and prayer as part of that process.

The tradition of the "quiet time" stresses the importance of the individual's time with God, time to read and study Scripture and pray. The Bible is a powerful book precisely because it points to Jesus and it teaches us the truth about God, and about ourselves. Willard writes, "If you bury yourself in Psalms, you emerge knowing God and understanding life."[2] Others would say the same of many other books of the Bible. The Bible is the primary witness to Christ, and it has an authority that other writings and other speech do not have, but the power is in the hearing of the word. It is those who are receptive to God's word who will be changed by it. Reading Scripture is useless if we do it simply out of duty, without listening or being willing to be changed by what we hear. In other words, it is not a magic formula, and just because we read the Bible every day does not mean that we will necessarily be changed. No doubt many of us have encountered men and women

2. Willard, *The Divine Conspiracy*, 75.

who religiously read their Bibles every day but who remain mean-spirited, judgmental, angry, and difficult. James writes, "Do not merely listen to the word, and so deceive yourselves. Do what it says" (Jas 1:22). Hearing God's word is transformative when we know we have everything to learn, and we are willing to follow what we hear.

HEARING AND LISTENING TO THE BIBLE

The Bible is not an easy book, and understanding Scripture takes time and effort. Jesus taught that we have to be those who listen and are attentive to his words, in order that we can put them into practice. At one point in our lives, we had six young men of different ages living in our house. I am hopeless at relinquishing control of the kitchen, and so for these months, the planning, buying, and cooking of food took up a large amount of my time. There was one time when I had to leave the house to run an errand, and so I left instructions with one particular boy about what food was to go on when, so that everything would be ready when I got back. When I returned, some of the tasks had been completed, but most had not. When I asked why they had not been done, the reply came, "Sorry, I heard but I wasn't listening." This nicely sums up my experience of living with lots of boys! Hearing and listening are very different. Listening moves us to respond.

In Luke 6, Jesus teaches his disciples that those who listen and respond to his words will be like those who build their houses on a firm foundation. Immediately after this, Luke records the story of the centurion who comes to Jesus to ask for healing for his dying servant. The centurion, even though he is Roman, and not Jewish, recognizes the authority of Jesus's words. He tells Jesus not to trouble to come to his house because he need only speak the word and his servant will be healed. Jesus is amazed at his faith. The centurion understood the power and the authority of the creative, life-giving words of Jesus, and was prepared to act on them.

In the parable of the sower, Jesus tells the story of the different soils on which the seed falls, which is really a story about how we receive the word of God. The seed sometimes falls on bad soil where it gets snatched away or dies, and sometimes on good soil, where it bears much fruit. Sometimes we fail to hear the word, and to act upon it, and it gets snatched away. Other times, the word sinks in and bears much fruit. In a commentary on this parable, Murray Rae writes, "The process of hearing the word involves, *essentially*, the fruitfulness of faithful discipleship, enabled by the Spirit, and ever dependent upon divine forbearance and grace." It is always because of God's grace and the power of the Spirit that we are enabled to listen and to obey, and when this happens, the result will be fruitful and faithful discipleship. Rae goes on to make the point that when we have become hearers of the word, we also in turn become bearers of the Word.[3] Those who hear the words of Jesus, and put them into practice for faithful discipleship, will in turn go out and make disciples.

Putting Jesus's words into practice is not an easy task, not something we learn to do overnight, and it is certainly not something we can or should do on our own. It is very good to develop the individual habit of daily Bible reading/listening, prayer, and worship. All these practices will contribute to the renewing of our minds. However, listening to God's voice, and acting upon it, is something we learn to do together, with the help of one another and within a worshipping community.

HEARING AND LISTENING TO THE PREACHER

We have been involved in one way or another with various new movements in the church, sometimes called Fresh Expressions, and sometimes called the emerging or missional church movement. It seems now that labels are elusive, and often prove to be largely unhelpful in communicating anything of value about the nature of any particular church. Whatever people end up calling it, there has been a new move in the Western church to plant churches that aim to reach out to people who are not walking through the doors of traditional churches on a Sunday morning. These churches take many different forms, meet at different times and venues, and are often not particularly recognizable as "church" as we have traditionally known it. I love the idea of diversity, of outreach, and of creativity in planting churches. Some of these churches really have succeeded in bringing the good news about Jesus to groups of people who would never set foot in a traditional church on a Sunday morning. This is a cause for real rejoicing.

It is disturbing, however, that so many people involved in these movements advocate abandoning the practice of preaching altogether. Is it really true that because our culture has changed so much the gift of preaching in the Western church is now redundant? I do not believe so. It is crucial, of course, that our preaching is relevant, lively, and applicable. It may be that we need to adapt our style of preaching to suit our cultural needs.

3. Rae, "Theological Interpretation," 13.

Preaching will be ineffective if it becomes boring or detached from our everyday lives. In this now somewhat amusing excerpt from Luther's works, he berates preachers who fail to reach their audiences, and speaks about the importance of preaching being accessible to ordinary people.

> Cursed be every preacher who aims at lofty topics in the church, looking for his own glory and selfishly desiring to please one individual or another. When I preach here I adapt myself to the circumstances of the common people. I don't look at the doctors and masters, of whom scarcely forty are present, but at the hundred or the thousand young people and children. It's to them that I preach, to them that I devote myself, for they too need to understand. If the others don't want to listen, they can leave . . . we preach in public for the sake of plain people. Christ could have taught in a profound way, but He wished to deliver His message with the utmost simplicity in order that common people might understand. Good God, there are sixteen-year-old girls, women, and farmers in the church, and they don't understand lofty matters.[4]

Poor sixteen-year-old girls, women, and farmers! But at least Luther thought they were worthy of attention and needed to be taught. Preaching is a spiritual gift, and an art, and through preaching, the truths of Scripture are brought to a gathered group in a way that brings life and hope.

Some men and women, and even children, have the spiritual gift of preaching. That is, they have the gift of speaking from and about the words of Scripture that brings out the meaning, brings them alive, and enables us to see how to apply those truths in our lives. They are able to communicate the truth of Scripture to their hearers in a way that bears fruit in people's lives. This ministry is incredibly valuable for the church and for the world. It is unbelievably short-sighted to think there is no longer any place for the expounding of Scripture, by someone who has the gift of preaching, for both believers and to non-believers. Preaching does not only have to happen in a twenty-five minute sermon on a Sunday morning, including three points beginning with "p." If a person has a gift of preaching, she or he will preach in any and every setting. When a preacher preaches, Scripture comes alive, and the hearers are inspired to act. Preaching in the form of explaining and applying the Scriptures is transformational. Luther also wrote this, "the preacher's mouth and the words that I hear are not his;

---

4. Pelikan and Lehmann, *Luther's Works*, 235, 383.

they are the words and the message of the Holy Spirit [through which] He works within me and thus He makes me holy."[5]

Rather than abandon preaching, we need a renewed vision for what preaching in the power of the Spirit can be: a gift from God for our transformation. I remember hearing a talk by R. T. Kendall shortly after his ministry had been deeply influenced by a group of prophetic people who ministered in his church. He spoke on the gift of prophetic preaching and the power of the preacher to transform individuals if he or she also listened to the Spirit to discern how the word of Scripture might be specifically applied to the hearers. When preachers preach prophetically, we often hear people responding by saying things like, "I felt like the preacher was speaking right to me," or "I felt I was the only person in the room." These encounters can be powerful and life-changing, and are for believers and non-believers alike. There are countless testimonies of people who have either never been to church, or have not been to church for years, walking into a church and hearing a sermon that was tailor-made for them. It touches the heart, and leads to repentance. God by his word, through the gift of preaching, brings life and hope.

Preaching also includes proclamation. Jesus came preaching (or proclaiming) that the kingdom of God was near. John the Baptist proclaimed that Jesus was the Lamb of God who takes away the sin of the world. Paul, Peter, Stephen, the early apostles, all preached and also proclaimed the truth about Jesus Christ in order that people would know the truth and the truth would set them free. In the Lutheran tradition, the preached word is *viva vox Dei*, the living voice of God. It generates faith, hope, and obedience. It can lead us to repentance, give us a vision for the future, and inspire us to set aside the distractions of the world, so we might seek first the kingdom of God. Moreover, there is something powerful in knowing the whole community is hearing the same word. Nick once preached in Zimbabwe on the need for Christians to respond to the terrible plight of those who were suffering from AIDS. Soon after his sermon, a small group of people came to him to say that they would like to do something, even though they were not quite sure at the time what that should be. In the weeks and months that followed, this small group of people established what they called the AIDS Task Force, which has grown into a wonderful and significant charity dedicated to the care, education, and welfare of families in Mabvuku (a high density suburb) who are affected by AIDS. It is still going today and is

5. Ibid., 24, 170.

run by highly efficient and dedicated teams of people who have affected the lives of hundreds of widows, grandparents, and orphans. This is an example of the power of the preached word, falling on good soil, and producing fruit a hundred times over.

HEARING AND LISTENING TO THE PROPHET

As God leads us by his Spirit, there are times when he will speak to us in ways that are new and surprising. He may give us a fresh way of understanding Scripture, a revelation about a particular situation, or a future plan or person, which will then alter the way we see things. God speaks to and through his people to teach us, lead us, and guide us. Listening to God's voice through the gift of prophecy is often precarious. We can never be 100 percent sure we have heard the voice of God, because we only know in part and we only prophesy in part. But hearing the voice of God through a prophetic word or a revelation reminds us that we are truly in a relationship with a living God who knows us, and everything about us, intimately. Sometimes we hear a promise of God through Scripture and we are called to act upon it. At other times we might receive a prophetic word, and in the same way, we are called to act upon it. Of course, these "words" must be weighed and tested. They must conform to the revelation that we have already received in the Bible. They must edify, comfort, and encourage. They must at all times lead us to be loving towards others.

In the times when I have believed God has spoken to me in this way, I feel both convinced I have heard the voice of God, and wholly sure I might be wrong. I have sometimes been wrong, and sometimes I have been right. I have felt so sure on some occasions that God is leading me in a particular direction, that I have changed my plans in order to accommodate this new God-given one. I would only ever do this with wise counsel and the prayers of others, but these times have been enormously significant for me in my journey of faith. When we step out and act as though the promises we have been given are real, we are molded into people who learn to listen for his voice and to trust him whatever our circumstances. We are changed when we hear wrongly and when we hear right, because in both instances we are learning to discern the voice of God. Jesus's life was shaped by the will of the Father. He did only what he saw the Father doing. For us, learning to listen to the voice of God, whether through the words of the Bible, a preached word, or a prophetic word, and obeying it, is how we begin to follow in his footsteps.

The gift of prophecy, like preaching, is a gift not just for the church, but also for those outside the church. Paul writes in 1 Corinthians:

> But if an unbeliever or someone who does not understand comes in while everybody is prophesying, he will be convinced by all that he is a sinner and will be judged by all, and the secrets of his heart will be laid bare. So he will fall down and worship God, exclaiming, "God is really among you!" (1 Cor 14:24–25)

LAYING DOWN MORE THAN THE LAW

In chapter 2, I spoke of the importance of knowing who we are as God's children before we can begin to know how to behave in Christlike ways. If we do not know who we are as God's sons and daughters, we will view the Christian life in terms of behaving in a certain way, or being "good" rather than as the joy of being free to become fully human in Christ. The burden of being "good" will become intolerable, and will lead either to deceit, discouragement, or rebellion. It is only in the power of the Spirit as he works in our lives that we are able to begin to conform to God's standards for relating to him and to one another. We will explore the work of the Spirit in chapter 4, but in this section we will study what Jesus taught about how we should relate to God and to one another in Matthew 5–7.

Jesus claimed the entire law could be summed up in two commandments: to love God with all your heart and all your soul and all your mind, and to love your neighbor as yourself (Matt 22:37–38). Jesus was a preacher and a healer, but he was also a teacher, and his teaching—which came through parables, stories, warnings, confrontations, proclamation, and revelation—all related to these two commandments. He was constantly teaching those around him how to do these two things: love God and love one another. In the Sermon on the Mount, we see Jesus's teaching on how to live out these two commandments in totally practical ways. He speaks of the stuff of everyday life: worries about money, fears about security, jealousy, anger, difficult relationships, straight talking, greed, sexuality, and the like. Jesus's teaching is about how to order our relationship with God and our relationships with one another so that we conform our characters to the character of God. If we, as the people of God, can reflect his character to the world, then we will be properly participating in his mission. We will be extending the mission of God through the church, demonstrating the truth about Jesus in our words and our deeds. This is Jesus's teaching on how to develop both the mind and the heart of Christ. In the middle of the Sermon on the Mount is the daunting phrase, "Be perfect, therefore, as your heavenly Father is perfect" (Matt 5:48). In some translations, it says, "be holy," meaning the same thing, although I am not sure which sounds more intimidating! Surely, it is not really possible to be perfect or to be holy in the way that God is holy. In the face of an impossible task we might feel defeated before we even start. Nevertheless, Jesus expects this of us, so what does it mean for us with our flawed, sinful, imperfect, and unholy lives to become holy, as God is holy?

At the heart of Jesus's teaching is an exhortation to order our relationships in truthful and loving ways, both in our relationship with God, our relationships with one another, and even in our relationship with material things. Jesus begins his teaching by declaring who, on this earth, are the truly blessed. Blessed are the poor in spirit, blessed are those who mourn, blessed are the meek, and blessed are those who hunger and thirst for righteousness. For some reason, I think we often misinterpret this to mean those who somehow have some semblance of holiness about them already. It sounds rather pious to be meek and to hunger and thirst for righteousness. But I do not think this is what Jesus meant at all. If we are really "poor" in spirit, we are poverty-stricken when it comes to spiritual things. We are the irreligious, the unholy, the spiritually bankrupt. Blessing rests on the spiritually needy. Blessing rests on those who know they have suffered loss. Blessing rests on those who are longing for the day when justice and righteousness triumphs over oppression and abuse, those who are longing for the life-giving presence of God. Jesus's mother, Mary, prophesied that with the birth of her son, the proud, the oppressors, and the rich would be sent away empty-handed, and the poor, the needy, and the humble would be filled to overflowing with the blessings of God, but there is no spiritual merit in being the poor and the needy. They are simply *the ones who know their need*. The only prerequisite, therefore, for the blessing of God, is that we understand our need of him. Jesus's teaching is only liberating and nourishing for those who know they are hungry and thirsty.

Jesus tells his hearers in the Sermon on the Mount that the purpose of following his teaching is in order to be "salt" and "light" to the world. Salt was a highly prized commodity in the ancient world. It was so essential to every part of life, and was so crucial for maintaining power that it sometimes said to have "made the world go round." To Jesus's hearers, salt would have been associated with both life and power, and known to have been a necessity for health and prosperity. Salt both heals and cleanses wounds, and preserves food from rottenness and decay. Light is similarly a powerful metaphor. Light brings safety and security, it exposes things as they really are and it dispels darkness. Jesus's vision for his followers is that they bring healing, life, and truth into the world, dispelling sickness, hunger, oppression, and captivity. The means by which he says they will be able to do this is to put his words into practice. The old law is not replaced by Jesus' new teaching, but surpassed by it. His new teaching requires not just following a set of rules, but a change of heart. He then describes what this will look like in practice.

SO ACTUALLY, WHAT WOULD JESUS DO?

Jesus goes on to describe what is at the heart of all the destruction that occurs in human relationships: anger, contempt, hatred, greed, lust, unforgiveness, betrayal, lies, manipulation, and revenge. His response is uncompromising —we are to reject every single one of these character traits in favor of the opposite response. If we are angry, we are to forgive and settle matters quickly. We are to refuse to use other human beings as objects for our own sexual gratification. We are to keep covenants and promises that we make, and not betray our marriage partners. We are to speak plainly and truthfully, and avoid manipulation and lies. We are to refuse to take revenge, and to love and bless those who hate us.

Jesus describes what this new way of living looks like in relation to God. Our personal acts of worship: giving to the needy, prayer, and fasting, are to be done in secret to guard against the temptation of needing to appear righteous in the eye of others. Our acts of worship and devotion are to come from our hearts, out of love for God, and not out of any need for recognition from those around us. God desires truthfulness and love to be at the heart of our relationships with one another and truthfulness and love to be at the heart of our relationship with him. What we do when nobody is looking is the only true measure of our love and devotion to God, and for this reason, Jesus urges us to nurture our life of worship in secret. If we start to go through the motions of piety for the sake of others, which is only too easy to do, then we have lost the heart of worship.

What of the obsession with material things that has gripped our culture? Jesus teaches that those who follow him need not be caught up in the worries about money, clothes, housing, or the future. This is a radical challenge for all of us living in the West. It is rare to meet Christians who really appear to be free of the burden and pressures of materialism. Jesus's answer to this is twofold. First, we are to give freely and generously. Second, we are to invest in his heavenly kingdom. Our money and our possessions are to be used freely to further God's kingdom, and not incessantly stored up for a rainy day, or to bolster our desperate need for security and status. It is very hard not to panic about the future, especially when we feel we are in a vulnerable position and those around us are secure and well off. The truth is, however, that none of us knows what the future will bring, and Jesus wisely points out that there is enough to worry about each day without adding to it by worrying about tomorrow.

All these life issues Jesus teaches on are extraordinarily relevant and contemporary. When we think about the Sermon on the Mount, we might imagine Jesus standing on a hillside in flowing robes addressing a huge crowd of first-century Jews, all listening and having to make sense of his teaching in their own context, but his teaching has an amazing contemporaneity for us today. How many families do we know where one member of the family is no longer speaking to another? How many people justify long-term anger and unforgiveness in their relationships on the grounds that they have been hard done by and ill-treated? People expect cover-ups and lies as part of everyday life and society—in work relationships, by politicians, bankers, criminals, school kids, the church, etc. Pornography and promiscuity are not only tolerated, but often celebrated as part of a sexually liberated society. Divorce is being made "easier" partly to ease the pain of a divorce, but also to accommodate the large number of divorces we now face. For people living in the West, it is almost impossible to escape the trap of materialism, the emphasis on "image" fueled by the fashion industry that affects both men and women, the sexualization of girls from a young age, the effects of broken families, and a whole host of issues in society that affect us all, all of the time.

If the church became a community that modeled a radically different way of relating to one other because we understand what it means to embody the character of God, the impact on society would be enormous. Christians living in the way Jesus describes would indeed be salt and light to society—life-giving, cleansing, healing, loving, and freeing. The Sermon on the Mount is not a set of guidelines about how we might be nice to each other, but it is a radical vision for society. Finally, however, Jesus gives a salutary warning: do not stand in judgement over others. If we learn to be a truthful and loving people, it is not in order to stand over others in self-righteous pride, but in order to serve the people around us. If we have encountered the grace to be free to love those who hate us, forgive those who hurt us, to love God with our whole hearts and minds, to be free from the grip of greed etc. then we must extend that grace to others. In chapter 5, we will explore in more detail how we might live this out in our relationships.

Notwithstanding that it is impossible for an individual to achieve perfection in this life, I do not believe these standards are entirely impossible for the church in some form. The most important proviso, however, is that we cannot achieve anything either on our own (in our own effort), or by ourselves (without the help of others). The Sermon on the Mount is not God's vision for individuals, but for the church. It is only as the people of God that we can even begin to reflect his character, and it is only through the gift of the Word and the Spirit that our hearts can be changed. We began this chapter by remembering that the gift of the Son is the gift of the Word, who with the Spirit is the powerful life-giving force behind everything that exists. If "abiding in Jesus" means being connected to this extraordinary power then of course he is able to re-create our hearts and our minds and reshape our desires so that our lives begin to look like his. We cannot entirely rid ourselves of envy, covetousness, anger, greed, hypocrisy, using others for our own sexual gratification, manipulation, lies, anger, unforgiveness, and all that prevents us from wholeness and health in our lives and relationships, but we can begin by recognizing the destructiveness of it for ourselves and our society. We can refuse to let it fester and grow. We can encourage one another to resist these things, and not to indulge them. Jesus's teachings are not really about "doing the right thing" but about being a people who reflect what is good and true and beautiful. The Sermon on the Mount is all about our characters and our hearts, and the way of life that Jesus describes is a way of joy and peace and freedom. Those who learn to live according to his words will find untold spiritual blessings. In Luke's Gospel, Jesus concludes his sermon by promising his disciples the gift of the Holy Spirit. In the next chapter, we will see how the gift of the Spirit works with the gift of the Son in the process of the transformation of the heart.

DYING AND RISING WITH CHRIST

In many Protestant traditions, we focus on the Word as the person of Christ, the word as Scripture, and the preaching of the word, but we often neglect the power of the presence of Christ with us in the sacraments. The two sacraments of baptism and the Eucharist are also given to us to bring about a renewal in our hearts and our minds and our bodies. In these two sacraments, we not only remember the life, death, and resurrection of Jesus, but we also act out a drama together, as we take part in these rituals in the church. We tell the story of death and life with our words and with our actions. Taking part in the drama of baptism and the Eucharist together has a powerful effect on a community. We declare the truths of our faith, we make promises to God and to one another, we remember the power of the cross and the resurrection, we remember God's promises to us, we pledge ourselves again to God's service, we act out our unity as the one body of Christ, and we receive his grace.

The physical acts of taking the bread and the wine, and of immersing or pouring on of water are more than just acts of remembrance and symbols of our faith. A symbol does not necessarily have to have anything to do with the thing that it symbolizes. It is just that we have all agreed that this particular symbol will mean that. Some symbols make more sense than others: a dove for peace, a balloon for a party, a raised fist for power. Others are completely random, like hand signals, which are polite in one country and offensive in another. The sacraments are not just symbols, randomly chosen, but signs— they have a connection with the thing they signify. Because of this, they act as formative agents for us in our lives of worship to God. Sometimes they are described as a visible means of invisible grace. God's grace works in and through them in our minds, hearts, and bodies.

I think of taking part in the sacraments as being like the bodily and physical side of relationships. All loving relationships are physical: friendships, parents and children, siblings, and lovers. We hug, kiss, cuddle, hold one another, and make love. Loving one another with our bodies both flows out of our love for one another, and strengthens the bonds between us at the same time. Physical affection and intimacy both come out of love and feed love at the same time, because we both give and receive. Submitting ourselves to baptism and taking part in communion regularly, is a physical act with a deeply spiritual significance. We give ourselves to God in worship and surrender, and we receive from him through the gifts of water, bread, and wine.

A few years ago, a young woman called Bea, who had good friends at our church, became a Christian. She was a student at Bristol University and she had been brought up with no church background whatsoever and had never been baptized. We did not have a church building at the time, but we happened to know some people then who had a swimming pool, and they kindly offered it and their home for Bea's baptism. We held a lovely party at their house one evening with lots of Bea's friends, many of whom were not Christians. We had lots of food, some worship, a short talk, and a chance for Bea to tell her story of why she wanted to be baptized. We then all processed out to the pool and amongst a funny mixture of laughter and reverence, we watched Bea go through this strange ritual of baptism in a floodlit pool. No doubt, it seemed a strange thing for many of the non-Christians there, but everyone seemed to appreciate that this was something deeply significant for Bea. I was standing next to her when one of her friends came to say goodbye. He gave her a big hug and said, "Wow Bea, I guess this is the end of an era!" He may not have known exactly why he thought that, but he could not have been more right. Kevin Vanhoozer writes this about baptism:

> Nothing draws us into the pattern of Jesus' communicative action more than the rite of baptism. Baptism marks our entry into the church, our regeneration and purification from sin (Acts 22:16). More important, baptism enacts our solidarity with Jesus' own death and resurrection; in baptism we participate in being buried with Jesus (united in death) and in being raised with Jesus (united in life).[6]

Vanhoozer brings out this dual aspect of baptism. We are not simply enacting our solidarity with Christ, but we are somehow *participating* in his death and resurrection. This will be part of how we are transformed by the person of Christ.

CELEBRATING DEATH

The Eucharist is often described in different ways: Holy Communion, communion, the Lord's Supper. And it is often celebrated in very different ways: formally and daily by a priest, only once or twice a year, as a meal around a table, with wafers, with bread, with wine, grape juice, etc. I am not speaking about the Eucharist as enacted in one particular way, simply as the ritual we take part in of sharing the bread and the wine together in remembrance of Jesus's death and resurrection. Taking part in the Eucharist is significant in so many ways, and I cannot begin to spell out in a short space, the depth and richness of the meaning of the Eucharist for the church. Jesus commanded his followers to break bread and to share wine in

6. Vanhoozer, *The Drama*, 75.

remembrance of him and of the new covenant that was fulfilled in his life, death, and resurrection. We do this because Jesus told us to, but how does taking part in the Eucharist make us more like him?

Pope Benedict XVI said this about the connection between abiding in Jesus and the Eucharist: "It seems to me that we must meditate deeply on this mystery, that is, that God makes himself Body, one with us; Blood, one with us; that we may abide in this mystery in communion with God himself, in this great history of love that is the history of true happiness. In meditating on this gift, God made himself one of us and at the same time he made us all one, a single vine."[7] God gives himself to us in Christ, and through Christ's death and resurrection, he unites us with himself. Through this he brings salvation, healing, and wholeness. It is this that we celebrate in the Eucharist. Moreover, we enact the unity of the body that is ours in Jesus.

The Eucharist is about salvation and unity. It is also, paradoxically, about both sacrifice and feasting. The Eucharist tells the story of Jesus's oneness with us as a human being and his sacrifice for us. Each time we take part in the Lord's Supper, we remember this, and we celebrate both the forgiveness of our sins as individuals, and our unity with him and with each other. But it is also something that we respond to with our own sacrifice of our lives once again, for him. In Romans 12:1, Paul writes, "Therefore, I urge you brothers and sisters, in view of God's mercy, to offer your bodies as living sacrifices, holy and pleasing to God—this is your spiritual act of worship." Of course, offering our bodies to God means offering all we do to him, but in taking communion, we are enacting that offering of worship, sacrifice, and surrender to him all over again. We give ourselves, and we receive him. As I was spelling out previously, the sacrificial giving of ourselves to God results in an abundance of his gifts to us, and this too is enacted in the Eucharist.

It is right that communion is reverent and prayerful and many people use the time of taking communion for individual reflection and repentance. However, when we only take part in Eucharistic services where it is all terribly solemn and quiet, we can forget that part of what we are doing is celebrating the life and liberation of being united with Jesus in his death *and* his resurrection. A non-Christian friend of mine once said to me, "I don't understand why everyone looks so miserable at communion. Surely you should be going up to communion on your knees, and then coming back down dancing?!" That has stayed with me for years. Like with Bea's friend,

7. Pope Benedict XVI, *Lectio Divina.*

it was the non-Christian's perspective on what we are doing as Christians that brought home to me just how meaningful these rituals are. I think we have yet to develop more ways of expressing the celebration and feasting that should also be part of communion.

In this chapter, we have explored how, through the gift of the Son, God makes us more like him. The truth of the incarnation, that God has walked this earth in Christ, is the mystery at the heart of our faith. We have so many ways of remembering this, of meditating upon it, celebrating it, living in the truth of it, and reminding one another of what it means for us. I have tried to bring out some of the ways we can allow God's gift of the Son and the Word to transform us into being like him. To conclude, I have listed a few holy habits, practical ways in which we can engage with the gift of God's word, in such a way that he will change us from within.

HOLY HABITS

Abiding in Jesus

The idea of "abiding in Jesus" is often described in terms of meditation. If meditation on the person of Christ is something that captures your imagination, then that is wonderful. If you do meditate, dwell on the truth that you are connected to the one who speaks and brings life out of nothing, who says a word, and brings the dead to life. We live in Christ, and he lives in us, which means, actually, that we cannot stay the same.

A second way of understanding what it means to "abide in Jesus" is simply just doing what he says. Mary told the servants at the wedding at Cana. "Do whatever he tells you." Whenever I have had the privilege of praying for someone who has just prayed a prayer of commitment to Jesus, I say the same thing to them, "And now you must do whatever he tells you to do." I say it to them because I wish that I lived like that myself. I feel we rarely live like this in the church. If we did, I believe we would see an almost unbelievable difference in the impact of the church in the world.

Secret Acts of Worship

Jesus expected his followers to give to the needy, to pray, and to fast. It is what we do when nobody is looking that counts.

Reading or Listening to the Bible

Reading the Bible is hard work. It requires time, effort, concentration, and application, especially if we want to be people who "listen." The Bible is not an easy book, but it is full of treasures and rewards for those who invest in it. The first thing to remember is to engage with Scripture as you can, and not as you can't. Here are some tips.

- If you are not good at reading, get the Bible in an audio format on your phone, ipod, or computer and listen to it being read.

- Regularly read the Gospels through to learn more and more about who Jesus is.

- Read the Bible out loud (other people will be blessed too!).

- Read the Bible with others.

We have a system in our church of "Pods," which we based on Neil Cole's "Life Transformation Groups."[8] People meet in twos or threes each month, having all read the same book of the Bible. They meet to discuss the book and pray together. The challenge is to begin to put into practice what they have read in the Bible. It is in Pods that we put into practice the advice that I found in one of my "Bible in a Year" books in relation to reading the Bible: trust the Bible, know the author, see the lasting principle, see the background, see the whole picture, value expert help, live it out.[9]

Memorize Scripture

I would love to be better at this because my experience of having heard the Bible recited, and not just read, is that there is an enormous difference in the effect that it has on the hearers. It is far more powerful to hear the Bible recited, than to hear it being read. I don't know why this should be, but it is. We encourage the members of our church to memorize Scripture and over the years, some have taken up this challenge with amazing commitment. I have heard the whole of Romans 8, Romans 12, Philippians 2, Galatians 5, 1 Corinthians 4, Psalm 139, and Psalm 103 all recited flawlessly by various individuals, as well as numerous smaller chunks by others. It is a wonderful experience.

8. See Cole, *Organic Church*.
9. Hughes and Partridge, *Cover to Cover Complete*.

Meditate on Scripture

Memorize a verse or two, and keep these words in your mind over a number of days. When you have a lull in your day, or just when you wake up or go to sleep, say the verses to yourself and ask God to show you what it means. This is a way of letting the word of Christ dwell in you richly. One person in our church keeps verses of Scripture as a "note" on his phone and told me that it's "great for times when I'm in a waiting for the bus and I'm bored."

Teach on a Passage of the Bible

Ask the people around you if you could share with them how God has been speaking to you through Scripture.

Respond to Scripture, a Sermon, or a Prophetic Word

If you believe God has spoken to you in some way and you feel challenged to act, then tell someone you trust and also write it down. This will be a way of reminding you to act upon it. Keep a record of what you feel God is saying to you and review it regularly.

Be Baptized

If you have never been baptized, consider making a public commitment to Christ in baptism. It is in baptism that we are both enacting our solidarity with Christ, and participating in his death and resurrection. It is also a powerful witness to those around us, as well as being something that we are told to do.

Participate in the Eucharist Regularly

It may be that you are not a member of a church where people share communion regularly, but communion does not always have to be a formal affair. Sometimes as a family, we simply share bread and wine together and read the Scriptures, remembering what Jesus has done for us. If you do take communion regularly in a church, consider dancing in response!

four

Formed by the Spirit

FREEDOM OF CHOICE

Paul writes in 2 Corinthians, "Now the Lord is the Spirit and where the Spirit of the Lord is there is freedom. And we, who with unveiled faces all reflect the Lord's glory, are being transformed into his likeness with ever increasing glory, which comes from the Lord, who is the Spirit" (2 Cor 3:18). Becoming like Jesus is a work of the Spirit in our lives, which brings us freedom. In chapter 1, we discussed the importance of following freely "the Christian stands, not under the dictatorship of a legalistic 'You ought,' but in the magnetic field of Christian freedom, under the empowering of the 'You may.'" The manner in which God works in our lives is not through coercion, but through wooing and winning. God loves us into obedience, and his will for us is that we obey Jesus's teachings because we are captivated by his person, not out of fear or duty. Christian freedom is very different from a worldly view of freedom because it is being freed to become Christlike, which in turn sets us free. This is a work of God brought about by the Word and the Spirit.

The secular, Western, individualistic view of freedom is completely different from the Christian view of freedom. If you were to ask someone in the West, "What is freedom?" they may answer that freedom is "being able to do otherwise" or they may refer to freedom of speech, political freedom, or intellectual freedom. These are important aspects of freedom. In addition to this, however, people will often reply along the lines that freedom is being able to do "what you want, when you want, where you want." Freedom has to do with choice, and often, seemingly, infinite choice. This concept of freedom, however, is one that, in reality, does not exist. There is no world, in fact, where any person is able to live like this. We have freedoms in the West that do not exist in other countries, but no human being anywhere is able to do *what* she wants, *when* she wants, and *where* she wants. We are all constrained by a multitude of conditions that prevent us from living in this way: laws, abilities, social convention, culture, other people, physical make up, natural laws, finances, age, expectations to name just a few. Furthermore, in reality, no one would want to live in a society where people did what they wanted whenever they wanted to. We appreciate the constraints that operate in society which prevent mayhem and anarchy.

I have often heard an analogy to illustrate this point, which goes as follows. One day, a guy turns up to referee a boys' soccer match, only to find that the person who was supposed to bring the boundary markers and the team t-shirts has not shown up. Everyone is waiting to begin, so he decides to start the match anyway, without any way of knowing who is on which team, and when the ball is "out." Needless to say, the match is a fiasco, with the boys getting angry and frustrated and the ref not knowing what to do. At half-time the person with the shirts and the boundary markers turns up, the match gets back on track, and everyone has a great time. The moral of the story is—rules are good, and everyone has a better time when we know what the rules are, where the boundaries markers are, and who is on which team. In other words, if we play by the rules, life is much happier. There is nothing wrong with the idea that rules bring freedom, because, as is well illustrated with this story, they clearly so often do. The problem with this analogy for the Christian life is that it only tells part of the story of freedom. Christian freedom is not really about following God's rules so that we can have more fun than the people who are not following God's rules. Many a youth worker has tried to convince their young people that this is true. The difficulty is that what the young people realize after a few years is that it just does not look like that. Their non-Christian peers, often lovely, thoughtful, and interesting people, actually are having fun, and it seems, anyway, are not suffering from all these terrible things that the youth workers tell them will happen if you do not play by God's rules.

The concept of Christian freedom is not actually about following God's rules or not following God's rules. It is about desire. The flawed definition of freedom that says it is doing what you want when you want is actually predicated on the idea that following your desires is always a good thing. It is a concept of freedom that has grown up in the context of a highly consumerist and individualist society. The Bible teaches that following our desires at all costs is ultimately a corrupting and often a terrifyingly destructive thing. Laws and rules are good in that they show us what is right and wrong, provide us with moral standards, and can be protective as well as restrictive. The problem with laws and rules is that they are powerless to change our desires. This is a matter of the heart. The Christian concept of freedom is that we are freed as our desires begin to conform to God's desires, for ourselves, and for others, and this is a work of the Spirit.

CHILDREN OF GOD

The Holy Spirit works in concert with the Word, effecting the transformation of our beings. He works, over time, in our minds, our spirits, our souls, and our bodies, enabling and empowering us to live our lives according to God's will. This will be a lifelong process, with most changes coming about slowly and deeply, rather than suddenly, or in an instant. Much of the time when we think about discipleship and what it means to be like Jesus, we think of the things that we *do*. We focus on the *practices* of discipleship: praying, studying Scripture, worship, sacrifice, etc. It is crucial to consider all of these practices, as long as we also know the principles behind them. If we are not sure of these, then we can so easily begin to think that it is what we *do* that will change us. Needless to say, what we do with our lives and how we behave is essential, and what we do really will change us, but we cannot begin here. Our understanding of what it means to become like Jesus begins with who we *are*, and not what we *do*.

We often talk about the "work" of the Spirit—in the world, in others, and in ourselves. Work is effort, initiative, and action. It is the Spirit, and not us, who works to conform us to the image of the Son. Our work, as we saw in chapter 1, is to respond to God's work in us, to engage with the dynamic of the kingdom of heaven, but the work that God does in us, and for us, should always be the primary focus, and the fount of all our understanding. If becoming like Jesus is not primarily about what we do, but about who we are, then who are we?

Those who put their trust in Jesus, are given the status of the Son in relation to the Father. We become children of God. The astonishing thing is that the New Testament writers describe this as not just a gift, but as a "right." Through faith in Christ, we have the *right* to become children of God (John 1:12). In all other aspects of life, Christians must be prepared to give up their "rights," and yet, we have one right left to claim. The Spirit is the one who brings that truth into our hearts and our minds, and who, at the same time, begins to transform us and to make it into a reality. He changes us from within, to make us like Jesus.

We cannot know we are God's children until the Holy Spirit reveals it to us. It is only by God's grace we are able to live in the truth of this—that we have the same status before the Father as the Son himself. We all—men, women, and children—are sons and daughters in the Son. Because of this we have the same rights, the same authority, and the same inheritance as Christ. The kingdom of heaven belongs to the children of God, and those who follow Jesus not only live with him, but will also reign with him (2 Tim 2:12). This reality is not something that is easy to grasp. All pastors know that the task of convincing people they are truly and deeply loved by God is a constant struggle. Many pastors, preachers, and ministers do not even know it themselves. The idea of unconditional love and boundless grace is not easy to understand. So many of us seem programmed to believe that love must be won or earned in some way, and the process of deconstructing this belief requires a great amount of teaching, love, and prayer. This message of unconditional love, of a love that cannot be earned, is at the heart of the gospel, and it is a message that one can only simply accept. We can and should remind one another of God's love, study the Scriptures, meditate on the love of Christ made known on the cross, encourage one another to reject the voices that chip away at our self-esteem and our confidence. All these are important spiritual disciplines, but it is only as the Spirit works in our lives that we will be truly convinced that there really is nothing we can do to be more beloved of God.

The Holy Spirit is the one who leads us to the knowledge that we are children of the Father and, moreover, that we are loved passionately by him. The grace and truth that comes in Jesus Christ is communicated to us by the Spirit. God pours out his love into our hearts by the power of the Spirit, so that we know we no longer need to live in fear or shame or doubt before God, but that we can approach him as ones who are deeply loved, because this is our right as one of his children. The Spirit shows us the reality of the cross: that because of Jesus's death and resurrection, the way has been opened for us to come to the Father. Jesus came to earth to reveal the boundless love of God for humanity. Jesus spoke to the disciples about the gift of the Spirit as the one who would come to carry on the work of God on earth after he had ascended. When Jesus himself was no longer with them in bodily form, the Spirit was sent at Pentecost in greater power than had previously been witnessed. At the Spirit's coming, the early disciples were empowered to preach the truth about Jesus, to do the works that he did, and to love one another as they had been loved by him. The message and the reality of the love and forgiveness of God in the life, death, and resurrection of Christ is spread abroad by the Spirit through the church.

The passionate love of God revealed in Christ is what the Spirit plants in our hearts. And it is this love, and this love only, that should compel the church outwards, towards the world. If I am loved so deeply, despite my faults, my weaknesses, my selfishness, then how much more am I moved to show love, forgiveness, and compassion to others. A love for others does not come from a sense of obligation, but from a realization, and a revelation that we ourselves are truly loved. Henri Nouwen writes this to his readers, as if from God himself: "All I want to say to you is 'You are the Beloved,' and all I hope is that you can hear these words as spoken to you with all the tenderness and force that love can hold. My only desire is to make these words reverberate in every corner of your being—'You are the Beloved.'"[1] When the Spirit touches our lives and our hearts, these are the words we hear from the Father. This is the primary work of the Spirit. And the knowledge of the love of God, that we are sons and daughters of the Father, will be the beginning of the renewal of our minds. It is then we will begin to see the world as Jesus sees the world. Who we understand ourselves to be is fundamental to our very personhood, and it is this love, and this love only, that should compel the church outwards.

CHILDREN IN A FAMILY

As we get older, we become increasingly aware of the significance of identity, and especially of family identity. People are fascinated by their roots and by their ancestry. It matters to us where we come from and who is in our family line, and there is no question that it adds to our own perception of who we think we are. Adopted children always face a hard choice—whether to try to find their biological parents for their sense of identity and heritage, or whether to accept the unknown, and that their roots now lie in their adopted family. Belonging to groups, cultures, and families gives us a sense

1. Nouwen, *Words*, 87.

of self and purpose. If we feel rootless and rejected, it affects every decision we make, whereas a sense of belonging and identity gives us confidence and security. It is what lies beneath our ability to act, to take initiatives, and to believe we are able to shape the world around us, rather than just be victims of circumstance. This can be used for good or ill, depending on the group we belong to, but the families, households, and communities we are part of shape our sense of self, and, in turn, affect the decisions we make in life. We will explore this more in depth in a later chapter when we consider the gift of community to transform us. Our new identity in Christ is to be part of a new family.

The work of the Spirit is not just for individuals, but it is to bring us into communities and the church family. This work of the Spirit goes on both inside and outside the church. The gift of the Spirit is for the church and for the world. Moreover, there is both a universal and particular aspect to the work of the Spirit in the world. The Spirit is the one who is working in us as individuals, revealing the love of the Father to us, and in so doing, making us more like Christ. He is also working in the church, forming the body of Christ into holiness, making us into the bride who is holy and blameless and pure. This is not just about "me and Jesus." This is about who we are together in Christ. Furthermore, the Spirit is working in the world, bringing creation, and the universe, to perfection. The universe exists because it is sustained by the power of the Word and the Spirit, without which, nothing would exist. God did not just launch the creation into being, and then leave it to run itself. God not only keeps everything that has life, alive, but more than this, he is moving creation to a goal, an end where creation will be perfected and God will be all in all. Although we cannot see it happening before us, the process of recreation has already begun. It began at the resurrection of Christ. God is recreating this world into a new heavens and a new earth, where the pain, struggle, torment, violence, and injustices of this world will be wiped away. The Spirit is constantly working to bring all of this about.

THE RIVER OF GOD

The Bible is clear that there is a powerful inevitability about the transforming work of the Spirit. This is true of his work in the world, in the church, and in us. Those who follow Jesus *will* become like him. As we have already noted, Paul claims that what has been predestined is that those who are adopted as sons and daughters will be conformed to the likeness of the Son. What has been predestined, decided beforehand, is that followers of Jesus will eventually look like him. "For those God foreknew he also *predestined to be conformed to the likeness of his Son,* that he might be the firstborn among many brothers" (Rom 8:29). This is the work of the Spirit in the life of a believer. "Now the Lord is the Spirit and where the Spirit of the Lord is there is freedom. And we, who with unveiled faces all reflect the Lord's glory, are being transformed into his likeness with ever increasing glory, which comes from the Lord, who is the Spirit."

When we lived in Zimbabwe, Nick and I went white-water rafting. I am terrified of strong currents and so have no idea why I decided to go. The force of the Zambezi is enormous, and I clung on to the side of our raft as we were buffeted through each rapid. It was comforting to be steered through the rapids by an experienced oarsman who, unlike me, had no fear at all, and clearly enjoyed every minute of it. In reality though, of course, even he had no power over the force of the river. He could judge the rapids, and steer us through them, but the truth was that we were all in the hands of something we had no control over. If you flip in the Zambezi, you can go with the movement of the river to arrive at a safe place on the bank, but the idea of working against the movement of the river is ludicrous. There is an aspect of the work of the Spirit in this world, and in our lives that is like this powerful river.

This is the picture that is given to Ezekiel in Ezekiel 47. Ezekiel is given a vision of water flowing out from the temple. As the water flows out eastwards, it gathers strength and depth. With each bend of the river, Ezekiel is led into deeper and deeper water until he can no longer stand, but only swim. Not only this, but as the river flows, it brings life: fish are teeming, trees are growing on the bank, and as it flows into the sea, it is so strong and deep that it makes even the salt water of the sea fresh. On the banks of the river, the trees never fail to bear fruit and in their fruitfulness, bring life and healing to the world. "[W]here the river flows, everything will live" (Ezek 47:9). One day, hundreds of years later, Jesus stood up in the temple at the feast of Pentecost and proclaimed in a loud voice, "If anyone is thirsty, let him come to me and drink. Whoever believes in me, as the Scripture has said, streams of living water will flow from within him." John explains, "By this he meant the Spirit whom those who believed in him were later to receive" (John 7:37–39). Jesus is referring back to Ezekiel's vision. It is he who is the temple, and the Spirit flows out from him to us, to the church, and to the world. There is something unstoppable, powerful, and inexorable about the move of the Spirit throughout history, through creation, and even in us.

Can we, as human beings, frustrate or thwart this powerful move of God in the world? In small ways, and for short periods of time, it appears we can. However, ultimately God's purposes for this world *will* be fulfilled. We, as human beings, are able to grieve the Spirit, we are able to resist him, or to refuse to acknowledge him. We cannot, however, and will not, *thwart* God's purposes for his creation. We know this from the work of God on the cross. The crucifixion of Christ was humanity's greatest attempt to extinguish God's presence; it is the ultimate manifestation of evil. When God himself—the perfection of love, goodness, and holiness—chose to come and live among us in Christ, he was loved for a while by a few, and then despised, mocked, spat on, and rejected. However, as humanity crucified Christ in our greatest attempt to extinguish God's presence with us, this became the very means by which his presence was and is being poured out on all flesh, bringing salvation to the world. Human beings can be powerful agents of destruction and wickedness in this world, but even in all of this, God's purposes for this world will be fulfilled. This power, this Spirit, is the one who is at work in us, bringing this about. It may not feel like it, and we may have days when this seems impossible, but it is true. Like all spiritual truths, we have to accept this by faith. Day by day, God is working in us by his Spirit to make us more like Christ, and this work carries on through everything we think, and say, and do, like a powerful river running its course to the sea.

JESUS AND THE SPIRIT

In chapter 2, we explored the transforming power of the Word of God in Christ. Jesus is the Word made flesh, the Son who walked among us. However, when Jesus came to earth, he was not only the Word who had become flesh, but he was also the Spirit-filled man. Jesus was baptized in the Spirit, filled with the Spirit, empowered by the Spirit and led by the Spirit. He lived his life on this earth, as the divine human being, who was also dependent on the power of the Spirit. He did not leave his divinity behind, or give it up, or even lay it aside, to become a mere human. He was still in very nature God on this earth, and the person of Jesus of Nazareth only existed because the divine Son took on a human nature. However, his Godhead was veiled, hidden in his humanity, and the life that he lived here on earth was one that he chose to live as we live, in weakness, vulnerability, and dependence. He chose not to be protected from the conditions of a human life by his divinity, but lived through a real human life with its trials and vicissitudes, even to death, in the power of the Spirit. When we read the Synoptic Gospels, we see constant references to the work of the Spirit in Jesus's life and ministry.

In the beginning, Jesus's very existence is brought about by the Spirit. He is conceived by the power of the Spirit (Matt 1:18; Luke 1:35). The Spirit is present at his dedication as a baby and later, the Spirit descends on Jesus in bodily form at his baptism (Luke 2:25–32; 3:21–22). At his baptism, even Jesus, as the divine Son, receives the affirmation and love of the Father in and through the power of the Spirit. As the Spirit comes on him, he hears the words of the Father, "This is my beloved Son; with him I am well pleased." After his water and Spirit baptism, it is the Spirit who leads (or, in some translations, "drives") Jesus into the wilderness before the start of his public ministry. In the desert, he overcomes the temptations of the devil and then returns to Galilee filled with the power of the Spirit. In Luke 4:18–19, Jesus identifies himself as the one who is anointed by the Spirit to preach the good news to the poor, to proclaim freedom for the prisoners, recovery of sight for the blind, and release for the oppressed. The work of the Spirit in Jesus is associated with the pouring out of the love of the Father, power, preaching the gospel, freedom for humanity, the defeat of evil and destruction, and holiness. Acts speaks of Jesus of Nazareth as the one "anointed with the Holy Spirit and with power, and of how he went about doing good and healing all who were oppressed by the devil, for God was with him" (Acts 10:38).

The Spirit was also Jesus's constant companion in his time on earth. The book of Hebrews, as well as stressing Jesus' unique divine status, also emphasizes the truth of his full humanity. He was like us, his brothers and sisters, in every respect (Heb 2:17). In his humanity, he was led through his suffering and death, but with the comfort and anointing of the Spirit. He offered himself up on the cross "through the eternal Spirit" (Heb 9:14); he cries to his Father, "Abba!" on the cross, also by the Spirit (Rom 8:15); and Romans 1:3–4 proclaims that the Son "was descended from David according to the flesh and was declared to be the Son of God with power according to the Spirit of holiness by resurrection from the dead." The Spirit is with Jesus throughout his time on earth, leading him, confirming his status as the beloved Son, and empowering him. The Bible refers over and over again to the work of the Spirit in the person and work of Christ: in his life, his ministry, and his death and resurrection. This is not to say that the Spirit replaces the divine nature of Christ, but that Jesus—the God-man—submits himself to the leading of the Spirit. The divine Son submits himself to a human life. This means that the life he lived, he lived as we live, in the flesh. Jesus' human life was not, therefore, pre-programmed by his divine nature. When Jesus is tempted, he chooses not to wield his divine power, but resists the temptations of the devil in the power of the Spirit and with the word of God. He developed as he grew from boyhood into manhood, through the enabling, empowering, and comforting work of the Spirit. This is crucial to our understanding of what it means to be a human being, and more specifically, what it means to be a follower of Jesus, and how we might even begin to be like him. We will explore this in the next section, but before we do, a word on how we are both like and unlike our Savior.

JESUS AND US: WHAT'S THE DIFFERENCE?

If Jesus is not only the Word made flesh, but also the Spirit-filled man, and there are parallels between his life and ours, does this mean that we can be just like him on this earth? It is reasonably common in charismatic and pentecostal circles to hear teaching along these lines: Jesus was a man filled with the Spirit; we are filled with the same Spirit, therefore we should be able to do all that Jesus did and, indeed, be like him in every way. Is this true? It is true that the same Spirit who anoints Jesus, anoints us. We are sons and daughters of the Father in the Son. We are baptized by the same Spirit. Moreover, we even participate in the divine nature (2 Pet 1:4). However, the work of the Spirit in the life of a believer is *analogous* and *not equivalent* to the work of the Spirit in the life of Christ. In other words, we know that the same Spirit who works in Jesus works in us. We also know that this same Spirit works in us in the same manner as he works in Jesus. We receive the Spirit in the *manner* that Jesus received the power of the Spirit here on earth—as one who fills and baptizes humanity. But the Spirit cannot work in us *to the same extent* that he works in Christ. Jesus, unlike us, is without sin and, therefore, never able to "grieve the Spirit" in the way that we are clearly able to do (Eph 4:30). Unlike us, his human will is never in conflict with or rebellion against the will of the Father, but always submitted and yielded to him. According to John 3:34, Jesus was given the Spirit *without measure*. He was the God-man filled with the fullness of God in every way; firstly because he was the divine Son who took on a frail human nature, thus transforming humanity, and secondly, because he was also filled fully with the Spirit. We cannot, in this life, replicate his life fully in this way.

Jesus is the natural Son and human beings are adopted sons and daughters in the Son. In addition, the Spirit in us is only the beginning of something that has yet to be fulfilled. The perfection that the Spirit brings, already realized in Christ, will only be fully realized in us when Christ returns, when this age is brought to an end, and the new age begins. "[N]ow we are children of God, and what we will be has not yet been made known. But we know that when he appears, we shall be like him, for we shall see him as he is" (1 John 3:2). In answer to the question, "Can we be wholly like Jesus on this earth?" we have to say "no." But are we able to *progress towards* Christlikeness in every way in the power of the Spirit? Yes. Jesus Christ was sinless in his humanity. He grew and progressed into maturity as a man, but remained sinless. We, however, undergo a process of sanctification, of growing in holiness, whereby we are constantly hampered by our sin. However, we can and do grow in holiness and in the empowering work of the Spirit, and this is his work in our lives.

JESUS: THE "MODEL" FOR HUMANITY

If we are both like Jesus and unlike Jesus, in what ways can we claim Jesus is a model for us, and how can we live up to this model? As we saw in the first two chapters, this is the question at the heart of discipleship. We have noted that different models or programs of discipleship will always select aspects of Jesus's life or ministry or character that we should imitate, or emulate. Moreover, individuals or churches inevitably stress one aspect more than another, depending on the life experiences, personalities, and biblical perspectives (among other things) of those who teach the programs and run the courses. None of us is immune to selecting some bits of Jesus's life and teaching, and leaving others out. But how is Jesus's Spirit-filled life a model for our own? Clearly, we cannot become itinerant Jewish rabbis from first-century Palestine, or even replicate any of the conditions under which Jesus lived and ministered. What was and is it about Jesus's life that is universally applicable to all people, at all times, in all places, regardless of history, gender, culture, race, age, etc.? I think the key lies in the relationship that Jesus had with the Father in the Spirit.

Jesus Christ is the perfection of humanity, the prototype of what it means to be truly human. His life lived on earth was lived in complete oneness with the Father. The Father's will was his will. The Father's love dwelt in him fully and without reserve. He only did what he saw the Father doing. And yet, this was not because he had been programmed to do this, or out of fear or duty, but because his love for the Father was so deep, and his knowledge of the Father was so perfect, that he would never have done otherwise. His eternal life was always thus. The Father, Son, and Spirit from eternity act as one because they are one. His life on earth, however, was lived in the same way, with all the works of God in this world as the work of the Trinity, but the Son was empowered in this by the Spirit. In his humanity, Jesus was free to respond to the Father in the power of the Spirit. This is the dynamic that is true of all human lives in relation to God. God's gift, his offer to us, is that we can respond to him of our own will and desire, in the power of the Spirit. As we do this, we are beginning to live in the way that Jesus lived over two thousand years ago.

The Bible teaches that the key to real human flourishing and freedom is in following Jesus. Jesus taught that about himself—that to follow him is life and joy and freedom—and the New Testament writers, and millions of Christians throughout history, have made this claim. The key to understanding this lays in one of the central ideas of the Christian faith, that humanity, men and women, are made in God's image. Despite hundreds of years of theological debate, we do not fully understand what that means, or which precise features of humanity bear the likeness of God, but we do know that humans bear the mark of their creator. We have been made by him, bearing his image, and in order that we can become like him in the fullness of time. It is an extraordinary concept that there is something of God in human beings, in the people who we live with, in the people we work with, in the people we are related to. Some teach that this image is destroyed by sin, others that it is only marred by sin. Whatever we believe, the church has always taught that it is only in Christ, and by the power of the Spirit, that this image can be fully restored. A human being truly and fully alive is the one in whom this image of God has been restored. Those who are truly free, are those who live in oneness with God's will. It will never happen in this life that all our desires and all our willing will be totally at one with God's will and his desire. We can, however, have moments, when our wills and our desires are brought into oneness and harmony with his. It is in these moments, the Bible claims, that we will be truly free. We will experience true freedom, and our humanity will realize its full potential. This is only possible in a restored relationship with God in Christ and in the power of the Spirit. Jesus, as God made man, had freedom to act and to obey, and this he did under the anointing of the Holy Spirit.[2] This is how his life is the model for our own. If Jesus is the picture of the perfect life, and becoming like him is the key to freedom and flourishing, what does that actually look like?

WHAT IS THE SPIRIT-FILLED LIFE?

In chapter 2 we explored the dynamic of cooperating with God's work of grace in our lives. We do not have the power to save ourselves, but we have been given the ability to respond to God's initiatives in our lives. Indeed, this response-ability is crucial for a dynamic and living relationship with God. Similarly, with the work of the Spirit in our lives, this grows and develops as we respond and cooperate with him and all he does. The Spirit forms us into Christlikeness in two ways: he shapes our characters and he gives us gifts. Both the shaping of our characters and the exercising of spiritual gifts is something that happens more fully for those who are willing to cooperate, than for those who are simply passive, or who actively resist God's work in their lives. Paul brings out the connection between the spiritual gifts and our characters in 1 Corinthians 13. Spiritual gifts are meant to operate only in the context of sacrificial and Christlike love.

The greatest threat to the work of the Spirit in our lives is sin. By sin here I mean the resistance to and rebellion against God's will. We can either actively and knowingly reject God's will, or we can simply refuse to acknowledge that God's will is significant or binding upon us in any way. We can ignore him. There is the sin of living as if God does not exist, and there are the sins that accompany that—behavior towards God and others that is ultimately self-centred. When we acknowledge Jesus as Savior and Lord, the sin of living for ourselves and not for God is totally forgiven and nullified. Our faith in Christ is all that is needed to be forgiven of all our wrongdoing and rebellion against God, past, present, and future. Painfully though, the sins of self-centeredness persist and are only slowly and haltingly dealt with as God transforms our inner selves. Even those of us who claim to "know" God, can live at times *as if* he does not exist, or *as if* what he says is not true. There is no Christian on this earth who does not experience the

2. I am indebted to Ivor Davidson for these insights. Davidson discusses the question of human agency, human flourishing, freedom, and the Spirit in his article, "Theologizing," 129–53.

power and the temptation of sin. We often shock ourselves by the ease with which we are able to contemplate unbelievably selfish, hateful, ugly, lustful, greedy, and envious thoughts. We are all capable of terrible, undisciplined and un-Christlike behavior. Human hearts are fragile and unpredictable centers at the core of our beings and the Bible is uncompromising about the capability of humans for destruction and evil. "For out of the heart come evil thoughts, murder, adultery, sexual immorality, theft, false testimony, slander" (Matt 15:19). "The heart is deceitful above all things and beyond cure. Who can understand it?" (Jer 17:9). Many people are affronted by the Bible's diagnosis of the human condition. Surely, human beings are essentially good? Surely, we can live "good" lives if we just try a bit harder? After all, some people protest, I have never murdered anyone, I have tried to love the people around me, and I live a good life.

Frustratingly, Jesus's standards for the "good" life are impossibly high, as we saw in chapter 3. Murder is not just sticking a knife in someone's heart, or shooting them point-blank. Murder is redefined as hatred, contempt for another, desire for revenge. Violence against another is not just physical, but is also desiring or coveting what they have. Generosity is not just giving away our surplus, but giving away when it costs us, and whenever there is a need. That is an extraordinary message in a society driven by materialism. Adultery is not just having sex with your best friend's husband, but fantasizing about having illicit sex, or lusting after others with your gaze. Just imagine what this means for us in a culture where the porn industry is thriving, and increasingly mainstream. Forgiveness is not just reserved for those who apologize to us, but must be given to those who hate us. Blessing is not just for our loved ones, but must be bestowed on those who damage us, and try to destroy us. These standards, in one sense, are ridiculously high, but they are not set so high in order to leave us discouraged and hopeless. They do, however, work as a shock tactic. They work as a means of revelation. They hold a mirror up to us, and to our inner lives. They convince us, in case we needed convincing, that in order to meet God's standards, we cannot possibly do it on our own, and that in order for our hearts to change, we need his power in us. We are wholly and utterly dependent upon God's goodness in us to live according to his will. The wonderful thing about the work of the Spirit is that his work in us transforms us so deeply that our very desires even begin to change. When this begins to happen there will be times when we no longer see the divide between "his will" and "my will" but it dawns on us that, in this particular time, over this particular issue, what he wills, we will also. These are the moments of greatest freedom and of being truly and fully alive.

One of the questions that occupies theologians is this: "Was Jesus not able to sin, or was he able not to sin?" Was he made in such a way, because he was also God, that even if he had wanted to sin, he could not possibly have done so. After all, Jesus was God and God cannot sin. Or was he able to sin when he suffered temptation, but remained sinless through his radical obedience to the Father? If we understand Jesus's human life as empowered and formed by the Spirit, in one way, we are able to answer both these questions in the same way. He may have been unable to sin because he was filled fully with the Spirit. He may have been enabled not to sin because he was filled fully with the Spirit. Whichever one we choose, if he is kept from sin by the Spirit, the enabling agent for his obedience and his sanctification is the Holy Spirit. It appears that the temptation for Jesus is to use his power as the Son of God in a way that will circumvent the cross. Jesus is tempted to exercise his divine power in his human life, in a way that he had chosen not to, by submitting to a human existence. In other words, in order for the temptations to be real, he must have still been able to exercise the power that was his as the divine Son, but he submitted to being formed in holiness and obedience in a human fashion, by the Spirit. The Holy Spirit sustains Jesus in his incarnate state as the holy and sinless one, and the most extraordinary and encouraging thing is that this same Spirit is at work in us. Obedience to the will of God is only imaginable, and becomes possible, by the empowering work of the Spirit.

A DIFFERENT FREEDOM OF CHOICE

What we see in the life of Jesus is that the work of the Spirit does not deny us our freedom. He does not control us and run our lives for us. He gives us *the freedom to agree with God*, and in agreeing with God, we become truly free. True freedom is not being free to do whatever I want. This is simply complete and utter selfishness. If I am able to do whatever I want, it means I never consider the consequences of my actions for others, and if I am not doing this, then I will be seriously trespassing on their freedom. In other words, it may feel free for me, but it is not the way to bring freedom to a community or a society. It can only have the opposite effect. The work of the Spirit is an enabling and an empowering Spirit to conform our wills to the will of God. In the garden of Gethsemane, we get a remarkable insight into the inner life of Christ. Here Jesus wrestles in his humanity with the path that he and the Father and the Spirit have chosen for him. The enormity of what lies before him seems to bear down on every particle of his being as he prays and cries out to the Father with loud cries. His body and mind and spirit are so distressed that he even sweats drops of blood. Jesus does not want to suffer and die. However, through his prayers and agony, in his communion with his Father, and through the power of the Spirit, he is brought to a place where he knows what he has to do, and he has the strength to do it. He goes to the cross for the joy set before him. He endures and triumphs over death.[3]

We are not able, in our own strength, to overcome the desires that war against God's desire and his will. Paul calls this the *sarx*, the "flesh" or, in some translations, the "sinful nature." The only power great enough to control the sinful nature is the Holy Spirit. In Romans 7, Paul describes the turmoil and the conflict of one who wants to do what is good and right in God's eyes, but finds that he or she cannot. "When I want to do good, evil is right there with me." When we try to keep laws, to be good in our own strength, we might be able to achieve a certain amount in our own strength, but ultimately, our minds and our bodies will fail us. We are unable to keep a strict rein on our desires, so as to conform "naturally" to God's will for our lives. So what hope do we have? Paul is convinced that through the forgiveness we receive in Christ, and the power of the Spirit, we can be released from this inner turmoil. There is a greater power at work in us against the destructive desires of the "sinful nature."

> Therefore there is now no condemnation for those who are in Christ Jesus, because through Christ Jesus the law of the Spirit of life set me free from the law of sin and death. For what the law was powerless to do in that it was weakened by the sinful nature, God

---

3. Orthodox theology teaches that Jesus has two wills: his divine will and his human will. Some people object to this on the grounds that it makes Jesus sound as if he could have been schizophrenic. The two wills of Christ, however, are the only way that we can make sense of the account of Jesus's struggle in Gethsemane. The question of Jesus's two natures and how they are related in one person is never going to be an easy one and theologians will never resolve once and for all how precisely to articulate this. An account of two wills for Christ, although seemingly difficult, is less problematic than proposing that there is only one will, as we would then have to postulate whether the one will was a human or a divine one. If Christ has only one divine will, then he cannot be fully human, and if only one human will, then he is less than divine. The idea that Christ has both a human and divine will in perfect harmony with one another and with the Father's will accords more fully with the biblical witness.

did by sending his own Son in the likeness of sinful man to be a sin
offering. And so he condemned sin in sinful man, in order that the
righteous requirements of the law might be fully met in us, who do
not live according to the sinful nature but according to the Spirit.
(Rom 8:1–4)

So what does it mean to live "according to the Spirit"? What is life in the
Spirit? It is not a sinless life, as that is not possible. When we say we have no
sin, we are deceived and are not telling the truth (1 John 1:8). A life that is
led by the Spirit is one that is reoriented towards God and not away from
him. This reorientation affects every aspect of our lives: our minds, our desires, our bodies, our hearts, our relationships, our hopes, and longings, etc.
The Spirit turns us towards Christ and, in doing so, teaches us how to relate
to the Father in the way that Jesus relates to him. As we relate to the Father
in the same manner as Jesus has taught us, the inner transformation begins.

LIVING BY THE SPIRIT

The Spirit changes our characters, gives us gifts, and leads us. Realistically,
the transformation of our characters is going to be a frustratingly slow process. We will often feel as if we take one step forward and two steps back,
or just that we make no progress at all. This is when we need to hold on to
the importance of the discipline of repentance and confession that we discussed in chapter 2. The daily practice of turning away from sin and turning
towards God, of putting off the old self and clothing ourselves with the new
is a powerful means by which the Spirit works in our lives. It is through this
that we are recreated to become loving creatures whose lives are oriented
around the Savior.

Secondly, a Spirit-filled life will be a life that is full of the gifts the Spirit
gives. The Spirit gives gifts to the church to enable us to live out lives that
witness to the goodness, power, forgiveness, love, and truth of Jesus Christ.
He gives us gifts of speaking the truth about God and preaching the good
news of God's kingdom. He gives us gifts of prayer and prophecy: speaking in tongues, revelation, vision, wisdom, and insight. He gives us gifts of
healing for the church and for the world: physical healing, spiritual healing,
and emotional healing. He gives us the gift of discernment: how we know
whether what we encounter comes under the authority of the Holy Spirit
or not. He gives us the gift of deliverance: to use the authority we have in
Christ to banish the powers of oppression and evil that harass and invade

our lives and this world. As well as this, he can give us practical gifts of administration, service, and organization and, furthermore, he is able to anoint our natural talents so that we can use them for God's glory. In other words, spiritual gifts are not always "spiritual," but can touch all aspects of life from sport to art, from business to farming, or a whole host of other pursuits.

There is nothing quite as extraordinary and exciting as growing in the gifts of the Spirit and in learning more about the way the Spirit fills us and leads us. I see the difference of being led by the Spirit and the rule-bound life as being like the difference between the person who follows a satnav, and the person who learns to be a tracker. Satnavs are enormously useful tools for getting us from A to B, without us having to use our brains, or any of our senses. We need no map-reading skills, no sense of direction, and no need to have any idea of where we are heading when we set off. We simply need a postcode, and a hope that the technology will not fail. Then we follow the instructions. Occasionally, however, the satnav leads us into a field in the middle of nowhere. Trackers have to find what they are looking for in a completely different way. People who learn to track have to spend hours out in the wild, or in the bush, watching for signs. Those wanting to learn to track are advised to find a special spot in the middle of nowhere, where they can just sit, and observe, for hours. They are encouraged to watch for little signs, leaves or twigs out of place, faint tracks, different smells. Trackers must use all their senses and become attuned to their surroundings. They must visit their spot frequently, over the period of a year, to understand how different nature is in different seasons. They must take notes, recording all their observations, learning with each one what their surroundings are telling them. Trackers must become sensitive to all the signs around them. They are seekers who learn to discern, to go on hunches and intuition, and to follow, sometimes, even the faintest of tracks. This is exactly what life in the Spirit is like. The more we become accustomed to the ways of the Spirit, the more we become confident to follow the signs God leaves us, to seek him in the ways he leads us. Christian maturity means growing out of satnavs. It means growing out of needing to be told what to do and where to go all the time. It means following willingly and happily, for the joy of working with the Father on this earth.

LISTENING TO GOD'S VOICE

When I was younger, I had an experience of a church for a little while where the emphasis was always on "doing the right thing," but with no teaching on the empowering work of the Spirit. There is absolutely nothing wrong with that if you can actually do it. I found I could not, so where did that leave me? It was not until I encountered the power of the Spirit, that I experienced the relief and the joy of knowing I was not expected to "do the right thing" on my own. Moreover, where I had never particularly wanted to live as a "good" Christian, as that all seemed far too dull, I suddenly experienced an overriding feeling of really wishing to please God. And this, not because I was frightened of him (although I feel, at times, in great awe of him) but because I loved him and I understood how true it is that he only wants the best for me. Becoming connected with the God who loves me, and experiencing the reality of his presence in the Holy Spirit changed everything for me. These insights have never left me. I still often feel that I am not very "good" and that I struggle to live as God wants me to, but fundamentally, I do not wish to displease God. I also know deep down, that I am not alone, and that my life is not a performance for God, but that he is with me every step of the way. Moreover, through the difficult and dry times, the memories of walking closely with God are strong, and they keep me wanting to stay near to him.

When we are connected to the life of God, we get a glimpse into his power, his creativity and his purposes for ourselves and for others. Let me just touch on prayer and the prophetic. It was a couple of years after I had been filled with the Spirit that I heard any formal teaching on the gift of prophecy. By then I was accustomed to "hearing God's voice." The teaching on prophecy made sense. I had experienced God communicating with me through my reading of Scripture, through pictures, dreams, and phrases that I would hear in my head, as if they were spoken to me by God. God was a living breathing presence in my life. I had no problems with that. When I read the Bible and the stories of the people in the Bible, hearing from God seemed normal. I know, however, that many people feel that "hearing God's voice" is a foreign concept, and like a closed book. I have no idea why some people seem to have no problem with certain spiritual gifts and others struggle with them. I meet hundreds of people who are so much more "gifted" than I am, both in the frequency and accuracy in how they hear from God and a multitude of other gifts. It is a mystery why some people seem to "excel" at some gifts while others of us get left behind. All I can say is that the best thing to do with spiritual gifts is to forget about other people, and just to ask for them. For example, I would love to see more people healed when I pray. I do not feel very good at praying for other people to be healed, but I just keep asking.

Personally, I see the gift of prophecy and revelation as very special, and so have always made an effort to learn from those who are more gifted in this area than me, and to encourage others to learn to hear God's voice. I recognize that there are a lot of potential problems with letting people loose to claim that they are hearing from God, and the gift of prophecy must be handled wisely and lovingly. On the other hand, Scripture warns us against quenching the work of the Spirit, and encourages us to eagerly desire the spiritual gifts, and especially the gift of prophecy. I view the gift of prophecy to the church, alongside the gift of preaching, as two of the most thrilling and humbling of the spiritual gifts.

God communicates with his people in many different ways and the gift of prophecy is seeing what God is doing or saying to individuals or groups at a specific time, in a specific place. It is personal and particular, and if loving and accurate, can be the source of immense comfort, encouragement, and wonder. Of course, we will only hear through our broken hearts and minds, so we will never hear perfectly, and what we say must always be held lightly and tested rigorously against Scripture. However, when the gift of prophecy really is used to encourage, comfort, and build up, it can be an amazing tool for drawing people close to God. It never ceases to astonish and delight me to realize that God uses us to speak to one another simply to remind us that he knows us, he loves us, and that our lives and times are held closely in his hands.

I have found, over the years, that most prophetic insight is given in order that we pray and intercede for others and their situations. Prayer is hard, but God gives us gifts to help us to pray. One is prophetic insight and the other is the gift of tongues. Both are spiritual gifts given by the Holy Spirit. Paul writes this of the work of the Holy Spirit and prayer: "In the same way, the Spirit helps us in our weakness. We do not know what we ought to pray for, but the Spirit himself intercedes for us with groans that words cannot express. And he who searches our hearts knows the mind of the Spirit, because the Spirit intercedes for the saints in accordance with God's will" (Rom 8:26–27). Some commentators, but not all, believe that when Paul writes of the "groans that are too deep for words" he is referring to the gift of tongues. Whether Paul is specifically referring to tongues here, which is unclear, we know from elsewhere in Paul's writings that the gift of tongues is a small but powerful gift of the Spirit to help us in our praying. The Spirit works in our minds, our hearts, and our spirit, teaching and helping us pray. He prays according to God's will, and the more we pray "in the Spirit" the more our prayers will be conformed to the will of God. The more we pray according to God's will, the more effective our prayers will be. The Spirit gives us the gift of tongues, and he gives us the gift of insight or revelation to show us how to pray in any given situation. I have often been praying in a particular way for a person, and then after I have prayed in tongues, I find I start to pray differently for them. I realize that what I was so "helpfully" praying beforehand is probably not what they needed me to pray at all. The Spirit is the only one who can give us God's perspective on others. If we rely just on our own perspectives, we may not be praying our best prayers for others.

BEING LIKE JESUS TO DO WHAT HE DID

Finally, life in the Spirit will mean being empowered to do the things that Jesus did. In John 14:12, Jesus tells his disciples, "I tell you the truth, anyone who has faith in me will do what I have been doing. He will do even greater things than these, because I am going to the Father." In some pentecostal and charismatic circles this verse is interpreted as if Jesus is saying to all individuals that they will perform greater miracles than he performed while he was here on earth. There is no greater miracle than the forgiveness of sins or the raising of the dead, so clearly Jesus did not mean this. I think it is right to understand the word "greater" to mean *quantity*, not quality, simply on the basis that if one has a ministry that lasts for seventy years as opposed to a ministry that lasted for three years, then this could be a plausible reading. However, if we bracket the question of "greater" for a moment, the simple reading is that Jesus is saying that faith in him (and only faith in him) will be a foundation for his disciples to do the works he did while on earth. For many this is a thrilling prospect. I have known men and women who have taken this principle to heart and pursued the works of Jesus on this earth: praying for miracles, healing, deliverance, even for the raising of the dead. Occasionally, this can become extreme, and I can quite see why others shy away from any teaching that our lives can indeed be used by God for great miracles. It can feel much safer (and certainly easier in some ways) to claim that these gifts are not for the church today, or just to steer clear of those with healing and deliverance ministries. However, in our churches throughout the years, Nick and I and our teams have always encouraged one another to seek the power of the Spirit in the lives of others, and have exhorted those with us to step out in faith in learning to do what Jesus did while on this earth.

Jesus comes to earth and nothing stays the same. The lame are healed, the blind see, the dead are raised. The kingdom of God breaking into the world brings profound healing and restoration, to individuals, communities, and even nations. We should expect that the coming of the Spirit upon people will bring transformation, and we should expect that the Spirit will work in us and through us, as a church, to bring this about. The message of the New Testament is that those who follow Jesus are empowered by the Spirit to continue the work of the kingdom on this earth. There is no reason to believe that this would cease for any reason. Our belief that God uses us, even in our frail and sinful lives, to restore others through emotional, spiritual, and physical healing sometimes means that we have been associated with movements or with people whose ideas we do not always agree with. We and any of our charismatic friends have been disturbed by triumphalist perspectives and teaching on miracles in some movements that is patently misleading. Teaching on healing must be balanced with teaching on suffering and what to do when prayers are not answered. The practice of deliverance should be low-key and private, preserving the dignity of the people who are prayed for. Claims that a person has been raised from the dead need to be tested and verified.

Believing, as we do, that when Jesus spoke these words to his disciples, he spoke the truth, and that this truth applies to the whole church for all time, and not simply to the apostles, means that as charismatics, we are identified with a churchmanship that sometimes places us with the weird and whacky. As a theologian, I struggle with this and, at times, I have been tempted to avoid the weird and the whacky altogether. The problem with this is that it is often in those places in the church that people really are being healed and lives really are being changed—probably not to the extent that we are led to believe, but nevertheless, change *is* happening. It is in these churches we find men, women, and children with great faith for the transforming power of the Holy Spirit to work in people's lives. Even with strange teaching, and some suspect practices in some parts of the church, which I believe we should address, there is something deeply attractive and uplifting about being with people who are full of faith for God to work, and moreover, to work through *them*.

EAGERLY DESIRING THE SPIRITUAL GIFTS

It is true that the use of spiritual gifts in a church requires a great amount of effort from the pastors to protect the church from possible misuse and abuse of the gifts. I am, therefore, sympathetic to those who are nervous of the possible damage of badly used spiritual gifts. Our experience, however, is that in the right context spiritual gifts can bring untold blessing to a church. I remember years ago hearing John Wimber, the founder of The Vineyard church movement, speak about how the healing ministry had developed in his church. He told the story about how, from his reading of Scripture, he became convinced that God heals today, and so he began to pray for healing for individuals in his services with laying on of hands. In the first year, nobody was healed. In the second year, some people began to be healed. In the third year, more, and so on. I do not know anyone who has pursued the gifts of the Spirit who has not grown in them. Furthermore, I am convinced that this is what we should be doing as a church, not for our own aggrandizement, but for the sake of the world. Not to seek spiritual gifts means that we are not seeking every possible way that we might be a blessing to others. If someone is sick, we will pray for their healing. If someone we know is suffering, and we do not know how to pray, we can pray in tongues. If someone we know is troubled and needs God's peace and comfort, we will ask God to speak to them through us. Exercising spiritual gifts is an extension of the love that has been poured out into our hearts that is meant to be poured out to others. Paul is very clear that sacrificial and Christlike love is the only acceptable context for spiritual gifts. If love is not the context, better that they are not exercised, but this is not a reason to extinguish them or ignore them. We must simply pray to be more loving, so that the gifts are rightly used. The spiritual gifts have been given to the church because God loves to bless us and he wants to use us to bless the world. We do not need to be hesitant about asking for spiritual gifts, because they are not for us, but for others. We are given gifts just to give them away. The more we ask for, the more we will have to give away. I cannot see any reason not to ask, not to be desiring, longingly and eagerly, countless ways to bring God's blessing to others.

LIFE IN THE SPIRIT: HOLY HABITS

What can we do to grow in the life of the Spirit? How do we respond to God's divine initiative of the gift of the Spirit? How can we live in ways that will make us more fully alive to the Spirit and more responsive to his leading? There are three main things that we can do: go on being filled with the Spirit, learn to hear the Spirit's promptings, and seek the gifts of the Spirit for the good of those around us.

Go on Being Filled with the Spirit

Pentecostal churches often teach that there is one main life-changing baptism of the Spirit, which is always accompanied by the gift of tongues. Indeed, the gift of tongues is viewed as *the* gift that authenticates the experience of being baptized in the Spirit, although this is not true of all Pentecostals everywhere. Charismatic churches teach that we should engage in a regular practice of praying to be filled with the Spirit, and this may or may not be marked by receiving the gift of tongues. In both traditions, the idea that we can and should pray to be filled or baptized in the Spirit is central. The filling of the Spirit is deemed to be the means of transformation and based on the model we have in the baptism of Jesus, in Pentecost, and in various accounts of the filling of the Spirit in the book of Acts—we pray for ourselves and one another, for this filling of the Spirit. Paul also takes up this idea, exhorting the Ephesians to "go on being filled with the Spirit" (Eph 5:18).

In our own church, we have a regular practice of praying for one another to be filled with the Holy Spirit. Sometimes, if a person feels that he or she has never experienced the filling of the Spirit, we will fast for a day with that person and then at the end of the day, we will pray for them to receive the Spirit in a greater and fuller way. Over the years, we have done this for a number of individuals, and it is remarkable to see the journeys that God has taken those people on since our day of prayer for them. Without exception, they are all involved with some significant ministry or other.

Why do we go on praying for one another aside from the exhortation that we read in Ephesians? I have often heard the phrase, "I leak." While I know that this is just meant to be slightly tongue in cheek, I do not think it is a helpful picture. The idea of "leaking" implies that whatever we do, the Spirit will somehow just inevitably run out, and so because of this, we have to keep asking. The Spirit does not inevitably "leak" out of us. What happens is that either out of apathy or deliberately, we all often close our hearts and our minds to the ongoing work of the Spirit. Living with God is dynamic and progressive. It is not a static relationship. All relationships need to be nurtured and fed and invested in: parent/child, friendships, marriage. None of these relationships deepen and grow if either or both parties cease to work at them. God never ceases to work at the relationship from his side, but we often do. We should not view the work of the Spirit as a continuous cycle of filling and leaking, but as incremental in our lives. We keep praying to be filled because there is more to learn, more to understand, deeper to go, higher to reach. There is no limit to the love of God and to the possibilities he creates in our lives. Being filled with the Spirit keeps us awake to those possibilities and the more we are filled, the more we are able to imagine what they might be and to live in the faith that they might come about.

Learn to Hear the Spirit's Promptings

When you read the book of Acts all the way through, you cannot help but be struck by the constant activity of the Spirit. He speaks, leads, convicts, inspires, empowers, baptizes, and gives visions, prophecies, and revelation. The early church was built on the anointing and the leading of the Spirit. Learning to respond to the Spirit's promptings takes a commitment to the idea that God speaks through the Spirit to the likes of you and me, and time to learn how he does it. We will never hear in a way that is unencumbered, pure, or clear. The leading of the Spirit will always be filtered through our own thoughts, desires, ideas, emotions, etc., and therefore the way that we hear God's voice will always be fallible and vulnerable. Sometimes we will just be plain wrong. But this does not mean we are useless or should give up. God in his extraordinary grace has chosen to partner with us. He entrusts us with his work in this world, and he desires to help us by leading and guiding us. Like the tracker who sits and watches, and observes closely, we have to develop our spiritual senses: our eyes, ears, our intuition. It helps to record what we feel God is saying and to go back and see where when we heard God's voice, and what that felt like. Over time, we will become attuned to the leading of the Spirit.

Seek the Gifts of the Spirit for the Good of Those around Us

Unfortunately, the only way to grow in the gifts of the Spirit is by trial and error. It would be so nice to grow without the errors, but they serve to grow us into maturity and keep us humble! If we want to grow in evangelism, we have to start speaking to people about Jesus. If we want to grow in prophecy, we have to start sharing what we think God might be saying. If we want to grow in the healing ministry, we have to start praying for the sick, and so on. The best context for this is in groups or teams with people we love and trust. First, build friendships, and then encourage one another to step out and take risks in learning about the gifts of the Spirit. I have heard countless testimonies over the years of groups that have seen God move in great power among them and through them, to others, because they were willing to step out in exploring the gifts of the Spirit.

five

Formed by Life

A TIME FOR EVERYTHING . . .

So far, we have explored the transformational work of the Son and the Spirit in our lives, and how we might respond to that. God works in us by the Son and the Spirit, and we respond by repentance, confession, humility, and engaging with the life of the Spirit. The life of apprenticeship to Jesus grows as we learn how to trust him more deeply and more fully, and to put his teaching into practice. The place where we learn to trust him is the concrete circumstances of life. We cannot put the words of Jesus into practice in the abstract, but only in our everyday lives and in our real relationships. And it is only in these places that his words will be really tested. It is only in real life we discover whether his promises are true or not. In the second half of the book, we will look at what this means. How does God use our circumstances and our relationships to teach us more about him, to deepen our trust in his unfailing goodness, and to make us like him?

The writer of Ecclesiastes reflects on the fact that there are countless different seasons in life, many of which require not just different responses from us but, in fact, the opposite response.

> There is a time for everything,
> and a season for every activity under heaven:
>
> a time to be born and a time to die,
> a time to plant and a time to uproot,
> a time to kill and a time to heal,

a time to tear down and a time to build,
a time to weep and a time to laugh,
a time to mourn and a time to dance,

a time to scatter stones and a time to gather them,
a time to embrace and a time to refrain,
a time to search and a time to give up,
a time to keep and a time to throw away,
a time to tear and a time to mend,
a time to be silent and a time to speak,
a time to love and a time to hate,
a time for war and a time for peace.
(Eccl 3:1–8)

Sometimes we find ourselves living in many different seasons at once. It could be that in the same moment somebody we love is dying, while another person we love is giving birth. We grieve and rejoice all at the same time. Life is full of both unexpected joys and unexpected tragedies, and in reality, we never really know what is around the corner, even though many of us live seemingly predictable lives.

Our circumstances are made up of situations that, to some extent, we are able to shape, and other situations that are beyond our control to affect in any way. There is a constant dynamic in our lives of things happening as a result of our actions, which others have to respond to, and things happening to us and around us, to which we have to respond. Many times the sheer randomness of events can be deeply disturbing and disorientating, and it leaves us with numerous questions about the nature of God's control and intervention in this world. It is not just the paradoxical and random nature of life that is disorientating, but the fact that so many things that happen are so cruel and horrifying. The presence of evil and suffering in the world is a constant challenge to the Christian on so many levels: pastorally, theologically, and intellectually. Is God in control? Can he intervene? If so, how, and what does that actually mean? Like the writer of Ecclesiastes, we search for meaning in life, and in our circumstances. Why did this happen? What does it mean? Can we make sense of it all?

Over the centuries, theologians and pastors have given many different answers to these questions, some more helpful than others. Those questions are important, and we should take time to explore them, but they will never be fully resolved to everyone's satisfaction. In this chapter we will not focus on the "why?" questions, but rather on the "what?" and the "how?" questions instead. As we go through life, encountering an enormous number of different situations and circumstances, we can and do ask ourselves "Why?" but we also need to ask, "What does God want for me in this particular circumstance?" and, "How should I respond?" In many ways, these will be more fruitful questions in our journey of apprenticeship.

THE FOUR SEASONS

In Romans 8:28, Paul writes, "And we know that in all things God works for the good of those who love him." This is in the context of describing the process by which God transforms those who love him into his own like-ness. God works *in all things* to make us more like him, which is precisely the good that he is bringing about. God works through the good and the bad, the joys and the woes, the delights and the tragedies, and the everyday stuff of life to conform us to his likeness. In our years of ministering in very different cultures and settings, I have observed patterns in people's lives of how God works in all circumstances, and these patterns are mirrored in the life of Jesus when he ministered on earth. We have seasons in life, where we go through different experiences with each other, and with God, and in these different seasons, God teaches us new truths about himself, about ourselves, and others. These seasons can be described as "the party," "the desert," "the battle," and "the victory." Unlike our natural seasons, these do not always follow successively. Sometimes we find ourselves in more than one season at once. However, identifying where we are, and learning how to respond in each season, can be enormously helpful in learning and growing through each one. If we know which "time" we are in, we will understand better what is required of us. In this chapter, I will describe the different seasons and then give suggestions of how we might respond in each one. As we have already explored in previous chapters, our response to the work of God in our lives is a part of what molds us and shapes us, as God works in all things to makes us more like the Son.

THE PARTY

In John's Gospel, Jesus begins his ministry at a party, and not just a party, but a wedding party. Jesus, with his family, attends a celebration and a feast, and when it looks like the party is about to flag because the wine is running out, his mother tells the servants that her son will fix it! Mary has complete faith in him, that he will be both able and willing to create more wine; and he does—gallons and gallons of it. And this is not just any wine, but a far far better wine than the one that had already been served. This miracle tells us so much about the nature of God, and so much about his nature that we often lose sight of. God loves parties, feasts, and celebrations. I love the fact that Jesus loved parties so much that he was accused of being a glutton and a drunkard. But even better than that, he was accused of being a glutton and drunkard who spent his time eating and drinking with tax collectors, prostitutes, and sinners. It is not exactly most people's idea of God. He is not a prudish, disapproving, judgemental old man, but the Father, Son, and Spirit who gives not just generously, but lavishly to his children and, more-over, to the people who feel they least deserve it. There is an abundance and an overflow of wine (and *wine*—not grape juice!) at the wedding, where there was also feasting, celebration, dancing, and joy.

There are seasons in our lives when we experience the abundant blessings of God, and when there is an overflow of gifts from him. In these seasons, we have more than we need and, in fact, more than we ask for. God sometimes demonstrates his abundant generosity in the outpouring of spiritual gifts upon a community. In Luke 10, Luke describes a spiritual party. Jesus sends out seventy-two of his disciples, and they come back to him, absolutely ecstatic having done what Jesus told them to do. They are hugely overexcited at the power they have witnessed for healing, de-liverance, and transformation. They discover that the power in the name of Jesus is awesome. "Lord," they tell him, "even the demons submit to us in your name!" Jesus is thrilled. Luke writes, "At that time Jesus, full of joy through the Holy Spirit, said, 'I praise you, Father, Lord of heaven and earth, because you have hidden these things from the wise and the learned, and revealed them to little children. Yes, Father, for this was your good pleasure'" (Luke 10:17–21). The disciples are full of joy, Jesus is full of joy, the Spirit is at work in power, and the Father is delighted.

It is hard to explain exactly why and how this should be, but it seems that there are times when "heaven is open." What I mean by that is that at times it seems as if everything we ask for in prayer is granted and blessings abound. The prophet Micah prophesies to the people of Israel that if they give to God the full tithe, then the floodgates of heaven will be opened and there will be so much blessing poured out that they will not be able to contain it. In the Old Testament, there is sometimes, although not always, a provisionality about God's abundant blessing. The people of God are told that giving to the poor, a penitent heart, a contrite spirit, a pure sacrifice, and an obedient life, will all be rewarded with abundant blessing. At other times, God just gives because he loves to give. He even gives to the unrighteous and the wicked. In the New Testament, there are no conditions attached to God's abundant and lavish giving. All God's children are entitled to the gifts of the Father, and it is only because of God's extreme generosity that we are able to give back to him, and to others, in an equally generous manner. It is not *our* attitudes or our faith that triggers the abundant giving of God, but *his* abundant giving that changes our attitudes. It is in view of his mercy, in the light of his love, as a result of his extraordinary sacrifice, and because this is all given *while* we are still sinners, that we are brought to our knees in repentance and love and praise. When we are in a season of feasting, we witness this most keenly.

Seasons of feasting are marked by tangible evidence of the transforming power of the kingdom of God. When Jesus came, announcing the good news that the kingdom of God was at hand, he stood up in the synagogue and said and here is what it will look like: the poor will hear the good news, the prisoners will be set free, the blind will see, the lame will walk, and people will experience the Lord's favor upon them. Our own experiences of the party, is that all these things happen. Prayers are answered, healings take place, people are saved, often dramatically, worship and praise spring up, people prophesy with power and accuracy, and there is an abundance of joy and laughter. Countless churches have stories of times in their history when there has been a party, when spontaneously and without much warning, God begins to move in much greater power among them. Mostly, when this happens, the people respond by meeting more frequently and for longer periods. And when they do meet, they are often overwhelmed by God's presence. These are sometimes called times of renewal or revival, and people will often travel thousands of miles to experience the power and the joy of God in a particular place. Just as in Luke 10, with the story of the mission of the seventy-two, there are times when the Spirit moves in power and we want to be part of it, because it is so exciting.

WHAT ABOUT MATERIAL BLESSINGS?

Many of us, quite rightly, are wary of anything that smacks of a prosperity gospels. The idea that Christians are entitled to material abundance and wealth by virtue of being God's children or by virtue of being "obedient" to him is misleading and harmful. To teach that we are able to claim a right to material prosperity, regardless of what that might mean for others, is impossible to square with Jesus's teachings. On the other hand, God is extravagantly generous in his nature, and we as a church should be able to mirror that to one another. The wine at the wedding of Cana was symbolic, but it was also real. It was real wine for a real party. We have often seen people receive material blessings, and sometimes these have been really large gifts—amazing holidays, money for holidays, beautiful gifts when they least expected them, checks through the post, cars, and even houses. We have also known enormous generosity from others in our own families. These gifts have been more than just fulfilling a basic need. They have been an overflow of provision.

We tend to say in these situations that God has provided for us, and it is true in many ways that it is God behind the provision. The truth is though it is a person or a group of people who have been moved to give out of the generosity in their hearts, and their thoughtfulness of others. The giving of material things is not purely just from God, otherwise why do some people have so much more than others? Giving is from us, one to another. Sadly, we in the West have not really begun to understand what giving to one another sacrificially and freely really means. Those of us who have "things" should be demonstrating both freedom from the grip of money and God's generous nature by giving not just cheerfully but hilariously (as Paul says in 2 Corinthians 9) to those who do not have. God is interested in our material well-being. In the story at the wedding of Cana, he demonstrates this by joining in the party and the giving of an abundance of choice wine. This is meant to be mirrored in the church by the radical and abundant giving of those who have to those who do not have. In any times of abundance we ever experience, our first response should be to give away.

SHARING WHAT WE HAVE

When we find ourselves in a time of abundance, there are various ways in which we can respond. It is easy to believe a blessing is being poured out among us because we first fulfilled certain conditions. We prayed hard, we worshipped more, we got ourselves "right with God" and with one another. I have no doubt that God blesses and rewards our seeking of him with a deeper knowledge and love of him, but there are no conditions attached to the seasons of feasting. God's gifts are given freely and indiscriminately, not on the basis of our merit or work, but on the basis of his love for us. It is only through the gift of the Spirit in the first place that we are moved to pray more, worship more, sort out our relationships, etc. If we find ourselves at the party, we will probably be fully aware of the fact that this is pure gift. The strange thing is that sometimes the outpouring of God's gifts does appear to be linked to faithful prayer and repentance, but often it is more the prayer that went on in previous generations, rather than our own prayers. It is very common to discover that there were people praying faithfully for God's kingdom to come long before we arrived. In the Christian life, we reap where others have sown, and we sow in order that others may reap. Our first response then, must be to share. Freely we have received, and so we freely give away.

When the Spirit is poured out in abundance on a gathered congregation there are various signs that we should expect to see. The first is that the abundant blessings of God are received in all humility and shared with equal abundance to anyone who comes. The second is that the people are transformed to become more like Jesus: loving and forgiving one another, submitting to one another, serving one another. The third is that it should spawn work among the poor and the needy. We saw in chapter 2 that Jesus only teaches on three activities his followers should engage in: prayer, fasting, and giving to the needy. These should all accompany an outpouring of the Spirit. The fourth is that barriers are broken down between social classes, ethnic groups, and men and women. Racism, classism, sexism, and discrimination of any kind should be erased. Years ago I heard an interview on the radio with a bishop from Rwanda. He spoke very movingly about the horror of the genocide that had gone on there in 1994. When he was asked whether anyone could have foreseen the genocide, he replied, yes, in hindsight, they should have known that there was something wrong at the heart of their society and their churches. The mark of this, as he saw it, was that despite a phenomenal revival in which thousands of Rwandans had become Christians, the Hutus and the Tutsis still did not worship together. They had a segregated church, along tribal lines. We cannot really be enjoying the party unless we have the sign that there is truly no segregation or distinction between races, genders, classes, ages, etc. No one should be excluded and invitations should be sent out far and wide.

It is at the party that we get a foretaste of the abundance of heaven, of the things to come. Paul talks about the Spirit as a downpayment, guaranteeing what is to come—our full inheritance. There is a lovely picture of this in Isaiah 55. The people of God are invited to come to him to feast on the richest of foods, on wine and milk that overflows. There is no cost, no money to pay, and the result is an outpouring of joy and peace. The times of feasting are a glimpse of the promises to come. At these times it is easy to trust in the goodness of God. It is easy to trust in his promises because there is so much evidence all around us that God will do what he says he will. Unfortunately, life is not that simple, or that good. Our lives are much more mixed than this, and we do not get to stay at the party. As much as we would like to, we find ourselves instead, moving from place to place and experiencing God in radically different ways and in very different circumstances. We so often equate a powerful experience of the Spirit with the pouring out of spiritual gifts, healings, and signs and wonders, but the work of the Spirit in our lives will be to lead us and accompany us, not only into abundance, but also into times of desperation, battle, and victory. When we are in a time of feasting, what are the holy habits that we should focus on and how can we respond? What are the ways in which God forms us in these seasons?

FEASTING: THE HOLY HABITS

Receiving and Thanksgiving

Simply receive the gifts God gives and be grateful. The practice of gratitude is something that we need to learn in times of abundance and in times of hardship. It shapes us as people if we are always thanking God for what he has given.

Giving

If we are in a position where God has given freely to us, our response will be one of wanting, in turn, to give away.

If we are in a feasting season in our communities or churches, this will also be a time of being able to give. We should give of our time, our resources, our energy, and our money. Communities in which God is pouring out his Spirit in this particular way, become oases for the weary and beacons of hope. It is lovely to see the people in the middle of these communities respond with hospitality and grace to those who visit, who feel in need of refreshment and some "new wine."

Learn to handle power

Jesus sent out the seventy-two and they returned with joy saying, "Lord, even the demons submit to us in your name!" The power of God can be a heady thing, but generally, human beings to do not handle power well. When God gifts a community with healings, powerful prophecies, deliverances, and signs and wonders, it is imperative that these gifts operate in a context of sacrificial love, wisdom, and humility. It is the name of Jesus that is powerful, and not us ourselves.

Unity

"Make every effort to keep the unity of the Spirit through the bond of peace" (Eph 4:3).

It sounds strange that we should have to constantly remind one another that we *must* be loving, and that we must not allow anything to divide us. Even in times of great abundance, we will be tempted to be careless of one another's needs. The Spirit gives us unity and we need to make every effort to keep it in the way we treat one another. In 1 Corinthians 13, Paul talks about the futility and emptiness of spiritual gifts and power if we do not love one another as Christ loves.

Storing Memories

It is really important in times of abundance to keep a record of what God has done. Like Joseph, who stored enough food to see Egypt and the surrounding nations through a seven-year famine, we need to store our remembrances of what God has done in our midst. When we then find ourselves in a time of famine and drought, we can remind ourselves and one another of who God is and how he works. This feeds and nourishes us when we are feeling spiritually dry and worn out.

SPENDING TIME IN THE DESERT

On the journey of learning unwavering trust in God the Father, we very often leave the party only to find ourselves in the desert, and this is one of the hardest places to be. The Bible is full of stories of the people of God, who in following him, find themselves for periods of time in the desert, in the wilderness, in exile, or in prison. Jesus spent time in the desert at the beginning of his ministry, and this too was a work of the Spirit in his life. Luke reports that Jesus "full of the Holy Spirit was driven by the Spirit into the desert" (Luke 4:1). It is in the desert that we are formed in ways we cannot be formed elsewhere, and normally it is in preparation for a work of God in and through us, for which we are being made ready. Moses spent forty years in the desert, tending sheep, before he was called to deliver the Hebrew people from slavery in Egypt. Joseph spent years in prison before being appointed to prominence in Egypt. David had many years in the wilderness, as a fugitive, as he waited to be appointed king. Elijah spent three years in the wilderness being fed by ravens and living in a cave. After this he went to stay with the widow of Zarephath, and ended up raising her son from the dead. John the Baptist came in from the desert to begin his ministry. The apostle Paul spent three years in Arabia in preparation for his missionary ministry, and subsequently had several years in prison at different stages. Despite various men and women in church history having literally taken themselves into the desert, or into extreme isolation, most of us, if we were given a choice, would never choose the desert. It would be so much nicer to stay at the party. But most Christians, at some point in their lives, find themselves left out of the party, and stuck in the desert. What does it feel like to be out in the wilderness? What does it achieve, and how should we respond?

We will experience many different emotions in the desert, but the overriding one will be isolation. This is inevitable, as one of the means by which God does his greatest work in us in the desert, is to isolate us. Sometimes this means that we also feel abandoned and rejected. Our pride will be hurt. Most of the time, some or even all of the things that we rely on in life for security will be taken away: money, friends, reputation, social standing, positions of responsibility. We will feel stripped back, exposed, vulnerable, and humiliated. We will face many fears, and many temptations and these will be very real. In the desert, or in prison, we only get our daily bread and nothing more. The abundance of the party is all gone, and like the manna in the wilderness, God feeds us just enough to keep us going, but there is nothing extra to hide away for the next day. Each day we wake up having to trust that there will be enough strength and provision for that day. Sometimes we will feel as if we are just existing, and not thriving at all, and the sense of abandonment by God can become acute. Sometimes we will have moments when we feel utterly crushed, and we will be unsure of how much more we can take. Desert times are times of apparent fruitlessness and barrenness. They are hard times to live through. How do we react at these times?

However long we spend in the desert, it will be far too long. In short, we hate it. Like the people of Israel who wandered in the desert for forty years, we will grumble and complain. We will whine and moan, and long for the day that is over. If you are in the desert, you will plead with God to let you out and deliver you from the pit you feel you have fallen into. You will read the Psalms more than any other book of the Bible, especially the ones that express longing, "How long, O Lord!" You will pray for people to come and promise you that it will be over soon, and if some pious friend helpfully points out that God is refining you, you will probably feel like punching him or her. This process of whining and moaning can go on for weeks or months or even years. Normally, we continue to moan until we realize God is doing something in us he cannot do if we had stayed at the party all the time. When we begin to realize the new thing he is doing in us is not what will happen *after* the desert, but precisely what is happening *in* the desert, then we find a certain peace about being there. Unlike the desert fathers and mothers who took themselves into the desert to avoid the world and to encounter God, I have not yet met a person who has been thrilled to be in the desert. There have been times, however, when I have witnessed people making the transition from fighting what God is doing to embracing it, and allowing a deep and lasting transformation to occur.

As an aside to what I have described, I wish to mention the medical condition of depression which I do not see as quite the same as being "in the desert," despite the fact that if a person is suffering from depression, then she or he will inevitably feel as if they are in a spiritual desert. Those who are experiencing any kind of spiritual desert need kind friends around them, and those who will pray for them regularly; however, those suffering from depression also need to be able to get help from the medical profession.

STRENGTH IN WEAKNESS

The irony about desert and prison times is that here we feel weak, vulnerable, and trapped, and yet it is in these times we are being made stronger and freer than we could ever be without them. They are, of course, refining

times (although it is easier to see that in others than ourselves!). The refining, however, is not because we are so "bad" and we need to be made
"good." The refining we undergo is to set us free. It is often hard for us to
associate good things with discipline, but the discipline of God only ever
springs from his love, his mercy, and his compassion, like the discipline
of a good coach, or a great music teacher. In Hebrews, we read, "Endure
hardship as discipline; God is treating you as sons. For what son is not
disciplined by his father? If you are not disciplined (and everyone under-
goes discipline), then you are illegitimate children and not true sons" (Heb
12:7). These sound like harsh words. No discipline is pleasant at the time,
but if God disciplines us, there is a point to it. If we lose sight of the fact that
God's discipline is the greatest privilege, and as a result of the deepest love,
and that it only exists to bring us to greater freedom, then we will hate it.
We will probably hate it anyway, but it will help if we remember the truths
brought out in the early chapters of being sons and daughters of God. If
this truth is embedded in our hearts and minds, then our reactions to times
of loneliness and hardship will be much better. Our worst reactions come
when we lose sight of God's love and believe that we have been abandoned
in some way. Times in the desert will be times of deep healing and releasing, but it will feel like the healing of a surgeon's knife. It will be horrible
and painful, but necessary. We will be healthier and stronger, even if we are
left feeling scarred for a while.

Times of disciplining and refining are times when we are freed from
sinful patterns of behavior, fear, and pride: the stumbling blocks to faith
and freedom. This means that we can feel horribly weak in the process
of becoming strong. God allows us to become weak in order to make us
strong. This is a mystery. The psalmist writes, "For you, O God, tested us;
you refined us like silver. You brought us into prison and laid burdens on
our backs. You let men ride over our heads; we went through fire and water,
but you brought us to a place of abundance" (Ps 66:10–12). We have to
learn to accept this by faith and to learn this from experience, because it
does not make sense to us as a concept. We are frightened of weakness
and vulnerability, and we shun it if we can, but God does not. He even em-
braced it for himself in order to come and be like us in every way. He chose
to set aside his power, his glory, and his strength to become one of us, so
that he could rescue us from all the powers of destruction, both in ourselves
and in this world. In God's mysterious ways, weakness is a means to power
and strength. So in the desert, we are confronted with our weaknesses. In

the desert, we face temptations, which by their natures, reveal to us where we are still weak and needy, where we are still sinful and proud, where we still need God's Spirit to come and help us. They show us where we need to be healed. Temptations humble us. We are not the perfect people we like to think we might be, and we are vulnerable like everyone else. We are also confronted with our fears, and this too can be a deeply humbling experience. But God only takes us away to show us these things, in order to heal and deliver us from them. In the desert we are rescued from our emotions like jealousy, hatred, and envy, which, if let loose, will destroy us and others.

It is very common, after a time in the desert to emerge feeling weaker and wounded, much like we do after an operation. In the months and years that follow, however, we will find we have been healed of many things, and we are stronger. We will find we are freer from the needs that used to drive us. We are more confident in God's power and his strength, and less confident in our own. We are more settled as people, and more peaceful in every circumstance. We will find we are less dependent on others for our sense of self, and less needy of approval and affirmation. Often we are purged of the fear of failure, or of the condemnation of others, or of destructive relationships. Isolation can have its benefits! I began this section on the desert by writing that the greatest defining feature of the desert or the prison will be loneliness and isolation. One of our greatest fears in the desert is that we have been abandoned by God, despite God's promise that he will never leave us or forsake us. It is often only over time in the wilderness, and sometimes in hindsight, that we understand God's constant companionship with us in all that we live through. It is sometimes only through the desert experience that the truth of God's constant and deep love for us is embedded in our hearts. It is here we learn to trust him in a completely different and necessary way from the way we learned at the party. Henri Nouwen, who writes with profound insight into times of suffering, says this about loneliness. "The more I think about loneliness, the more I think that the wound of loneliness is like the Grand Canyon—a deep incision which has become an inexhaustible source of beauty and self-understanding. . . .The Christian way of life does not take away our loneliness; it protects and cherishes it as a precious gift."[1]

1. Nouwen, *Words*, 1.

PATIENCE IS A VIRTUE . . .

Because we find we are constantly waiting on God in the desert, it is here we learn patience in a new way. If we are used to getting what we want when we want, we will never learn the practice of patience and of waiting on God. The practice of waiting on God is an active, and not a passive pursuit. We wait for him, in expectation that he will fulfil his promises to us, and so we live in the concrete hope of his promises. This is not a practice we learn overnight, and is formed in us by the doing of it. Unfortunately for us, the only way to learn how to be patient is to experience being constantly thwarted and frustrated, which in itself is infuriating! Patience, however, liberates us to a new way of being, helping us to be peaceful while we wait for an outcome, and building our dependence on and trust in God. Impatience leads us to try to fulfill our desires in our own way, often leading to catastrophic results. Patience does not mean being inert, but it means refusing to force through an outcome or a solution when there is no obvious way ahead. It means waiting for God to reveal his solution and accepting that this will be for the best. Learning to wait on God, which is active and not passive waiting, is a way of learning more and more about him, and how he acts in this world. It draws us closer to God, and gives us deeper wisdom and revelation.

ACCEPTING THE THINGS WE CANNOT CHANGE?

One of the challenges we face in learning how God is working and how we should respond, is to know when we must wait and when we must push ahead. Are we searching or are we giving up? Are we fighting or are we yielding? Which season are we in? Making the right call is hard, and expending energy fighting for something that is never going to happen is exhausting and discouraging. Discerning God's will in any given circumstance can be enormously challenging, and is, of course, a gift given by the Spirit. It is precisely the process of being transformed into Christlikeness that gives us the ability to do this. Paul tells the Romans, "Do not conform any longer to the pattern of this world, but be transformed by the renewing of your mind. Then you will be able to test and approve what God's will is— his good, pleasing, and perfect will" (Rom 12:2). We begin to understand God's will because he gives us new ways of thinking and discerning. We will see the world as Jesus sees the world. In the desert or in prison, God teaches us how to hear his voice, he gives us new understanding of his ways and his character. Our own understanding often fails and we are called, instead, to lean on him and to trust in his ways, which are different from ours. In the next section, we will look at what it means to be in a battle and discerning God's will in those places. The desert is one form of a battle, but is characterized more by having to accept our circumstances, and accepting that they are being given to us in order to change us from within. Alcoholics Anonymous use a prayer that is an adaptation of a prayer by Reinhold Niebuhr. "God grant us the serenity to accept the things we cannot change, courage to change the things we can, and wisdom to know the difference." This is a great prayer for when we find ourselves in the desert.

THE DESERT: THE HOLY HABITS

Give Us Today Our Daily Bread

When we are in the desert, we will only have enough to keep us going for each day. We only get as much as we need with nothing left over. We have to learn first to be grateful for what we have, and second, how to trust that, despite not being able to store up for tomorrow, God will provide.

Praise and Thanksgiving

If we are in the desert, we will know the struggle of practicing daily praise and thanksgiving. The Bible speaks of a "sacrifice" of praise given to God, and when we are feeling that he has placed us on an anvil, in order to refine us, it will certainly feel like a sacrifice to praise and thank him in all circumstances. However, it is impossible to overemphasize this as a practice—to praise and thank God for his blessings, especially when we least feel like it. Praise and thanksgiving lifts our souls and our spirits, and helps us to recall the loving and gracious character of God.

Feeding on More Than Bread

When Jesus was in the desert, he practiced the discipline of living not on bread, but on the word of God, and this was his power in the temptations. In the desert, we have to learn to feed on God's word, and there will be great power in this for us. As we saw in chapter 3, this does not necessarily mean an hour of intense Bible study every day. Feeding on God's word might mean listening to the Bible, meditating on a verse, learning Scripture with a friend, singing the psalms, or however we find it easiest to internalize Scripture.

Remembrance

Practice the discipline of remembering who God is and what he has done. This is when you will need your prayer journals, and the stories of what God has done in your life before your time in the desert. It is important to rehearse God's promises and to remember them before others. In 1 Sam 7:12–14, Samuel sets up a stone, an "ebenezer" signifying a way of remembering that God had helped them to defeat the Philistines. Markers of how God has helped us in the past remind us that he is still with us and keep us hopeful that he will help us again in the future.

HE TRAINS MY HANDS FOR BATTLE . . . (PS 18:34)

I was an adult when I first read the four Gospels all the way through, one after another, and I was amazed at the person of Jesus I encountered there. For years, as someone who was not particularly well versed in the Bible, I had imagined Jesus to be something that, quite frankly, he was not. He was not as "nice" as I thought he was! Jesus was an extraordinarily more powerful person than I had realized—in every way. He was powerfully authoritative in the way he spoke and taught. He was powerfully compassionate in his dealings with the poor and sick. He was powerfully challenging to the rulers and leaders of his day. He was powerfully subversive. He was powerfully wise in his responses to his enemies. He was powerful in the way he healed and forgave, and restored those around him. He was powerful when he commanded Lazarus back to life. In addition to this, what also struck me, and surprised me at this time, was how much his life was marked by conflict. As the Prince of Peace, his life on earth was not exactly peaceful and tranquil.

There are many stories of conflict in the Bible, and many stories where conflict is played out between people groups, tribes, and individuals in terrible murders and bloodshed. The message of the New Testament, however, is that when Christians are drawn into conflict with others, they should not respond with violent retaliation or revenge, or, in fact, *any* retaliation or revenge. The reason for this is that when we find ourselves in conflict with others, the reality is that the conflict is not a human one, but a spiritual one, and therefore the battle must be fought on a spiritual plane. Paul writes in 2 Corinthians 10:3: "For though we live in the world, we do not wage war as the world does. The weapons we fight with are not the weapons of the world. On the contrary they have divine power to demolish strongholds." Similarly, in Paul's letter to the Ephesians, he exhorts them to arm themselves with spiritual armor against the devil's schemes because their enemy is not to be found in other people, but comes against them in the spiritual forces of evil in the heavenly realms. To fight against these spiritual forces, and to stand against them requires the full armor of God: his Word, his Spirit, the assurance of salvation, a trust in his good purposes, the truth of the gospel, and the power of constant prayer (Eph 6:10–18).

DIFFERENT BATTLES

There are four types of spiritual battle in the Christian life: personal battles against the sinful nature; the battles of hardship and suffering; the battles we fight to maintain loving relationships; and battles of intercession. These are not spiritual battles because they are purely spiritual concerns. They are not "spiritual" concerns, in a strict sense, because they are to do with the stuff of life. They are spiritual battles because they require spiritual solutions. The only way to "win" against destruction and despair in each of these circumstances is to follow Jesus's teaching and to put it into practice. Then we will not be defeated in the battles.

The first category, personal battles against what Paul calls the "sinful nature," are often the battles we encounter and fight in the desert. It is in this way that the desert is also a place of battle. Jesus fought battles in the desert against the devil, and although he was kept from sin by the divine nature and the Spirit, he clearly had very real temptations. These temptations were very personal to him. In our own personal battles, we will be confronted with our fears, our weaknesses, our temptations, and these will be very different from the fears, temptations, and weaknesses of others. First Peter 2:11 describes sinful desires as desires that "war against the soul." All of us give into sinful desires all the time, but the closer we draw to Jesus and the more attuned we become to the work of his Spirit, the more this will cause unease and disturbances in our own minds and souls and spirits. We have already discussed in previous chapters the gifts God has given us in order to allow him to fight these battles in us. He gives us his Word and his Spirit to bring our desires into line with his, and the way that we cooperate with the work of God in us is through repentance, humility, etc.

The second type of battle we fight is in the experience of hardship and suffering. The spiritual battle of continuing to live the life of unwavering faith and trust in God at these times is immense. We will have to battle to declare God's goodness, to have faith in his unfailing love, and to praise him and thank him in all circumstances. When we experience long-term sickness, caring for a special needs child, acts of violence and hatred, long term unemployment, seeing loved ones suffer, premature deaths, and countless other difficult situations, we are called, as Christians, to continue along the road of loving and worshipping God in all our circumstances. We are called to persevere and to endure, to love our enemies, to pray for those who persecute us, to offer our bodies as living sacrifices, and to take up our cross daily. The stresses and traumas of life can, at times, be overwhelming. In these times, we will need one another more than at any other time. We are very often carried through the battle by others who help us stay faithful through hardship and suffering.

The disorientation of these experiences can be profound. We tell ourselves, and others, that we follow and worship an infinitely loving God and yet, we live with terrible pain. There is no real way for us to make sense of most of what happens in these times. This is where the "why" questions fail us. The only thing we can do is to ask God the "what" and the "how" questions. *What* is God doing in and through the hardship and suffering to redeem the situation, and *how* might I respond? Years ago, I heard a preacher speak on hardship and the spiritual battle, and he made the point that Paul, in Ephesians 6, does not talk about doing any more than just standing. "To stand," he said, "is victory." Often we will feel that we have been defeated because life is just too hard, but hanging in there with God is powerful. Standing just means holding your ground. If this is all that we can do, then that is the triumph. Others standing and praying with us help us to do this. If we personally are not in a battle, one of the good things we can do is to find someone who is and stand with them.

The temptations in these times, like in the desert times, will be to believe we have been abandoned by God, that he does not care any more, or somehow we have failed. Persistence in trusting in God's goodness, in his good plans, and in his infinite care of all our needs is the biggest battle. We can only win at this if we are in communities that, themselves, are loving and caring, and where those around us demonstrate this love to us. It is important to keep reminding ourselves and each other of the truths enshrined in Scripture, but if they are not embodied in our communities they can truly appear useless. Telling someone God loves them despite the terrible hardship they are suffering is a poor substitute for showing them the love of God in practical support and care. Perseverance and praise through hardship and suffering is not something we are able to do as individuals, but is something we can only do as a community. The third battle we find ourselves in all the time within our communities, is the battle to maintain loving relationships, and we will discuss this in detail in chapter 6.

YOUR KINGDOM COME . . .

The fourth type of battle we are called to engage in is the battle of intercession and prayer. All Christians are called to pray in all circumstances. Paul even speaks of praying continuously (1 Thess 5:17), and all Christians are called to pray for God's kingdom to come and for his will to be done on earth as it is in heaven. One of the mysteries of our faith is the extent to which prayer actually does change situations? Does God do what he was going to do anyway? Is he just waiting for us to change, so that we will what he wills? We do not know how much of a part we play in the coming of God's kingdom on this earth through prayer, but we do know that we do play a part in some way, whether that is because we are changed as individuals and communities, or whether situations are radically changed around us. Prayer is powerful, and situations change as a result of prayer. When we are faced with the knowledge that God's rule and reign has not yet become a reality, and what that means for the world, we are moved and compelled to pray. When we have a vision of the healing, the wholeness, the liberation, and the joy that God's kingdom brings, then seeking his kingdom in the transformation of ourselves, and others, becomes something that we find ourselves constantly longing for.

Whether we conceive of evil as an identifiable or personal force, or as a total lack of goodness and a lack of the presence of God, destructive forces operate through us as individuals, through institutions and even through whole communities. The Bible describes the work of Satan or the devil as murder, destruction, division, lies, and theft. So when families begin to destroy each other, when church families divide bitterly over an issue, when people "bite and devour" each other, when the poor are oppressed, when children are abused, when people get lost to addictions and destructive behavior—all these occasions require us to fight a spiritual battle. The spiritual battle is fought with spiritual weapons, and our greatest weapon is prayer. Some have the gift of intercession. They have a great burden and enormous stamina to pray for long periods of time, and for seemingly intractable situations. These people will often be called to intercede for God's kingdom to come in situations of severe conflict or large-scale tragedy. They are able to pray, in faith, for major issues such as wars, national conflicts, drug cartels, child soldiers, the slave trade, sex slaves, pedophile rings, etc. Generally, intercessors pray for longer and on a much larger scale than most of us, and cannot understand why others are not moved to pray without ceasing. Samuel Chadwick, an intercessor, wrote this: "It would seem as if the biggest thing in God's universe is a man who prays. There is only one thing more amazing, that is, man knowing this, should not pray."[2] Intercessors in the Bible include Moses, Elijah, Isaiah, Daniel, Nehemiah, Jesus, Anna, and Epaphras. There are many men in the Western evangelical tradition who are known for their ability to pray: John Wesley, George Whitefield, Charles Finney, William Booth, Praying Hyde, and Rees Howells to name a few. There have, however, been millions of unknown intercessors throughout history, and so many of them are women. There are countless groups of women who get together to pray in groups around the world, some official and others just small prayer groups that meet every week. These groups of women are powerful in the spiritual battle.

Most of us do not pray at this level and, in fact, may very well struggle even to know how to begin to pray for anything of such enormity. All of us can pray though, as long as we find how we, personally, are able to pray. There are numerous ways and places to pray: kneeling, sitting, lying, running, walking, listening to music, in the bath, washing up, writing, drawing, praying Scripture, praying through liturgy, praying in tongues, praying with others, on our own, over the phone, skype, and the list goes on. There are also countless situations to pray for. We do not need to feel guilty because we cannot pray for world peace. Keeping the peace with our own families and neighbors is enough of a spiritual battle, and needs much prayer! When we are battling in a particular situation, it often helps to fast as well. I have included an appendix on the practice of fasting because it is such an enormously helpful and powerful gift with prayer.

2. Chadwick, *The Path*, 11–12.

Before I go on to outline the holy habits that help us to respond in battles, I wish to talk about the last season—that of victory or triumph. Although I believe all battles will eventually end in victory, it is not always the case we experience that in this life. On the other hand, there are times when we do see this in a very tangible way, and these times give us hope that out of terrible destruction, evil, hardship, and suffering can come great goodness, healing, and redemption.

THE VICTORY

The victory is when the hardships we face are the very means of the glory of God in our lives. It is when the suffering or the difficulty we experience is itself transformed into something powerful and wonderful, and beyond our expectations, for us and other people. The first and greatest example of this for us is in the death of Christ on the cross. Jesus was not glorified in spite of the cross, but *through* the cross. His suffering and death was the *means* by which he was glorified, and the very means by which God brought salvation to humanity. Calvin describes this in the following way: "Hence it is not without cause that Paul magnificently celebrates the triumph which Christ obtained upon the cross, as if the cross, the symbol of ignominy, had been converted into a triumphal chariot" (*Institutes* II.16.6). The pattern of the cross is then lived out in the lives of believers.

One example of this from the New Testament is when Paul and Silas are in prison in Acts 16. Paul and Silas are imprisoned for preaching the gospel. They are stripped, beaten, and severely flogged. At midnight, after all of that, they are praying and singing hymns to God in the prison, at which point they witness a miracle. Suddenly, there is a violent earthquake, the prison doors fly open and everybody's chains fall off. Paul prevents the jailer killing himself, and as a result, he presents himself to Paul crying out, "What must I do to be saved?" The jailer is converted dramatically and baptized with his whole household. He feeds Paul and Silas, and washes their wounds. The suffering and imprisonment of Paul and Silas leads directly to the salvation of the jailer and his whole household. The victory is when we are able to say, "without this, that would never have happened." Moreover, because our perspective is changed in this way, we are able even to thank God for the bad things, because they are the means to the good things. The suffering is the means to the glory. When the most difficult events become the means for something good, we then reinterpret the past, and sufferings and hardships are transformed in our minds.

As I have already said, most of us do not always feel as if we see this happening. There are times when we are left with bitter disappointments, and a profound sense of the futility and senselessness of suffering. Sometimes though, it is almost as if we catch a glimpse of what the redemption and re-creation of the world is going to look like. Jesus, astonishingly, went to the cross for the joy set before him. He must have glimpsed the joy that was to come, despite knowing he had to suffer. We cannot know this truth naturally, but we can only know the hope we have because that knowledge is given to us by the Spirit. Again, this is a spiritual truth that is spiritually discerned. It comes to us through the renewing of our minds. It is this knowledge and hope that causes Paul's outpouring in Romans 8, where we see his utter assurance that whatever we suffer in this life will be nothing compared to the glory that will be revealed in us when we become like Christ. We will not simply witness the glory of God, but we will *be* the glory of God. The followers of Christ, who become like him through suffering and the transformation brought about by the Spirit, will embody God's glory. This is what the whole creation is longing for. Until then, Paul is convinced that whatever we suffer, *nothing* can separate us from the immense and invincible love of Christ because the real spiritual battle has already been decisively and finally won.

THE BATTLE AND THE VICTORY: HOLY HABITS

Be Prepared for Hardship

If we are responsible for teaching or training others, the best thing we can do for them, is to prepare them for hardship. The Bible is clear that the Christian life is not a cushy option. It helps us to know this at the outset.

> Acts 14:23:"We must go through many hardships to enter the kingdom of God."

> Acts 20:22: "And now, compelled by the Spirit, I am going to Jerusalem, not knowing what will happen to me there. I only know that in every city the Holy Spirit warns me that prison and hardships are facing me. However, I consider my life worth nothing to me, if only I may finish the race and complete the task the Lord

Jesus has given me—the task of testifying to the gospel of God's grace."

Put On the Whole Armor of God

Study Ephesians 6, and pray through the different aspects of the "armor" that God has given in order to fight the spiritual battle. In the first three chapters, I have spelled out in different ways what this looks like in practice.

Join Forces

However hard it might be to sustain, do not stop meeting together, but work even harder to spend time with supportive, faithful, and prayerful friends, especially if they are friends who can make you laugh!

Remember That Jesus Has Won

Do not be discouraged by everything that you see before you. Find verses that encourage you to remember that God is powerful and mighty to save. These are a few:

> "But thanks be to God who always leads us in triumphal procession in Christ and through us spreads everywhere the fragrance of the knowledge of him." (2 Cor 2:14)

> "And having disarmed the powers and authorities, he made a public spectacle of them, triumphing over them by the cross." (Col 2:15)

> "If God is for us, then who can be against us?" (Rom 8:31)

> "The Lord is my light and my salvation—whom shall I fear? The Lord is the stronghold of my life—of whom shall I be afraid?" (Ps 27:1)

Lament

There are some people who are genuinely joyful people, but we should not feel that we have to be "jolly" all the time, as this can become wearing and false. There are appropriate times for mourning and lament, and a strong biblical tradition of expressing sadness at times of loss and death. Mourning can only lead to dancing if we go through the lamenting first.

Meditate on Romans 8

Romans 8 is one of the most wonderful chapters in the whole Bible on God's unfailing love for us.

LOSERS OR WINNERS?

Living through the four seasons of life can be very disorientating if we are not prepared for what is to come. Even if we are prepared, it can be confusing to know that God sometimes works in seemingly paradoxical ways with no apparent reasons. We began with a quote from Ecclesiastes. Later in the book, the writer of Ecclesiastes writes this:

> As you do not know the path of the wind,
> or how the body is formed in a mother's womb,
> so you cannot understand the work of God,
> the Maker of all things.
> Sow your seed in the morning,
> and at evening let not your hands be idle,
> for you do not know which will succeed,
> whether this or that,
> or whether both will do equally well. (Eccl 11:5–6)

Jesus told Nicodemus that the Spirit blows where he will. It is like the wind, you hear its sound, but you cannot tell where it comes from or where it is going. Following the leading of the Spirit in the Christian life, strangely, can be both a profoundly centering experience and a deeply disorientating one. Centering, because the Spirit leads us to Christ, and the closer we draw to Jesus, the more grounded, the more peaceful, and the more whole we become as human beings. Disorientating, because we will be led in ways we cannot predict, and into situations where we are constantly challenged to learn new things, about God and about ourselves. We should not be surprised to be disorientated and "wrong-footed" by the Spirit. He constantly breaks and remolds our view of God, dismantling the perspectives that have become warped and distorted, and bringing fresh and new perspectives on who God is "for us."

We love to feel we are in control, but however much we wish we could control our environment, and however much we make every effort to do just that, the circumstances of life are not predictable. We really have very little control of our world. Those who live in the developing world know this much more starkly than those of us who live in the affluent West. There are no magic formulas or programs we can follow that will guarantee how things will go. As we walk through the Christian life, sometimes we will feel like winners and at other times we will feel like losers, and God allows us to experience both. One of the great problems for us in learning how to respond to different circumstances is that it is very difficult to break a mind-set that tells us that obedience leads to blessing and prosperity, and disobedience leads to misfortune. This is one of the great difficulties that lies behind dealing with the hard times, because deep down we feel that those who are experiencing the "good times" must be the blessed ones. We have to learn to be both winners and losers, and to understand the work of the Spirit in both. Paul writes this, "I know what it is to be in need, and I know what it is to have plenty. I have learned the secret of being content in any and every situation, whether well fed or hungry, whether living in plenty or in want. I can do everything through him who gives me strength" (Phil 4:12–13).

What we are in control of, with God's help, is our responses to our circumstances. Paul learned the *secret* of being content in any and every situation. That is an astonishing claim when you think of the dissatisfaction that plagues so many of us. What is Paul's secret? It probably cannot be summed up in a short paragraph, but I think it has something to do with Paul's deep knowledge of who God is, in Christ, and the leading of the Spirit. Paul writes in Romans that he is utterly convinced there is nothing in heaven and earth that can separate us from the love of Christ; that there is nothing in the whole universe that can come between us and God because of the love poured out into us from the Father through Christ and the Spirit. He is also convinced that God will work through every and any circumstance for our good. This "good" is the good of conforming us to the image and likeness of Christ. That is the good God is bringing about, both for us and for the world. He is able to do this through any and every circumstance. Henri Nouwen writes, "The deep truth is that our human suffering need not be an obstacle to the joy and peace we so desire, but can become, instead, the means to it. The great secret of the spiritual life, the life of the Beloved Sons and Daughters of God, is that everything we live, be it gladness or sadness, joy or pain, health or illness, can all be part of the journey toward the full realization of our humanity."[3]

KNOWING WHERE WE ARE

I began this chapter with a quote from Ecclesiastes about the "seasons" of life. Knowing what God is doing in every season helps us live through each season, but it is not always easy to know where we are. When do we search, and when do we keep? Is it a time for building up, or tearing down? Do we let go, or do we cling on? Do we fight our circumstances or do we submit to them? There are no easy answers to these questions. The only way of answering them is to hone our skills of listening to the Word and the Spirit. It is how we develop our tracking skills that will lead us to know what to do and how to respond in different circumstances. One of the tensions that affects charismatic and pentecostal Christians specifically is to know how much and how long to pray for change, and when to let go. In the charismatic church, we teach a gospel of transformation for any and every aspect of life. God can heal our bodies, our minds, our emotions, and our spirits. God can transform family lives, relationships, and desires. God can deliver us from fears, addictions, and destructive behavior patterns. We believe not only that God *can* do these things, but that he *wants* to do these things. We have seen these changes with our very own eyes, and experienced them in our lives. What happens, then, when he doesn't do it? How do we explain it? How do we live it? And how do we know when to lay aside all our hopes and trust God for the outcome. I often reflect on the fact that it is easier to have a *que será, será* theology in life (whatever will be, will be) than to have a theology of transformation, and then not to see it always "work." The potential for disappointment is vast.

It may be easier, in some ways, to have a theology that leads to a passive acceptance of all aspects of human existence, but I do not believe that this is the fullness of the Christian life that Jesus taught about to his followers. God will undoubtedly accomplish every plan and purpose he has for the universe, but I also believe that he wishes to engage us in those plans, so that we begin to understand what a life lived for eternity will be like. This life is the beginning of eternity, but it is only the beginning, and actually, a very short one. It is the beginning, however, of becoming truly human, and of being set free to become more and more like Christ. We do not know

3. Nouwen, *Words*, 2.

the path of the wind, or where the Spirit will lead us, but we are capable of sowing. We can work in God's kingdom, as he has asked us to do. Paul calls himself a "co-laborer" with Christ. We are ambassadors, coworkers, servants, friends, partners with God in his work in this world. In Matthew's Gospel, Jesus says:

> Do not store up for yourselves treasures on earth, where moth and rust destroy, and where thieves break in and steal. But store up for yourselves treasures in heaven, where moth and rust do not destroy, and where thieves do not break in and steal. For where your treasure is, there your heart will be also. (6:19–21)

In all and each of our circumstances, we are given the ability by God to invest in his kingdom. Sometimes this investment will feel very costly. We will labor and labor and see very little reward. At other times, we will reap rewards that go far beyond our little hopes and dreams. We accept, in faith, that both sowing and reaping is storing up treasure. The deeper we are immersed in Scripture, and the great truths and promises given to us in the Bible, the more resources we will have to navigate the contours and unexpected turns of life. The more sensitive we are to the Spirit, and to the whisper of God's voice and his promises, the greater our ability to know what is expected of us in each and every circumstance.

I will never forget being in a small meeting in Zimbabwe years ago, where a friend of ours, Costa Mitchell, was speaking and leading. At the end of the meeting he had a number of very accurate and very healing prophetic words for individuals. After that, he invited people up for prayer. There was a family there who had a little girl who had a disease of the eyes. She had gone blind in one eye and was going blind in the other. Costa invited a number of people to come and pray for this little girl. After about an hour, she began to see better out of one of her eyes. Costa said he believed she was going to be healed and the group should carry on praying for her until that happened. We were not in the small group of pray-ers, so after a while, we left. We later heard that after about four hours the little girl was completely healed in both eyes. We know that Costa is not the sort of person who would claim God heals everyone all the time, but in this instance, he believed God would heal this little girl and he was right. He listened to the Spirit, who blows where he wills, and he encouraged that little group to pray into the night for her healing. That family's life was transformed by God.

WALKING THROUGH LIFE TOGETHER

One of the sadnesses for me about my own church tradition and culture is that we seem to be inherently self-obsessed in our church life. In our worship and prayer, it really is, so often, "all about me." Individuals matter, and our individual lives matter to God, but one of the ways we grow through our circumstances is to remember we are never the only people involved, and our responses to our circumstances will affect others for good or ill. In the next chapter, we will look at the life of apprenticeship in community, how we are both responsible *to* and responsible *for* those around us. Our situations and our circumstances always affect others as well as ourselves, and are so much more easy to live through with the help of those around us. We can ask ourselves and one another, what is God doing in this for *us*, and how does he want *us* to respond? We then make sense of our circumstances in the light of this, and discern what God is calling us to do. Knowing our identity both as individual sons and daughters, and as the body of Christ together, forms the bedrock of knowing how to respond in all circumstances.

six

Formed by One Another

THE PEOPLE OF GOD

G OD CREATED HUMANITY TO exist in relation to himself and in relation to one another. Even God himself is a relational being. He is one God who is also a triune God, and as Father, Son, and Spirit, God exists as one and three—three persons who relate in mutual love to one another. God's purpose for humanity is to bring all humankind into a restored and loving relationship with him, and into loving and self-giving relationships with one another, modeled for us by the life of Christ. There is no such thing, therefore, as an isolated or an individual existence. Human beings are created to be in relationship with their creator, and only exist in relation to one another. Moreover, the message of the gospel is that the only way of living a fully human and fully free existence is to be in relationship with God through Christ, which then enables us to relate to one another in ways that are truly self-giving and marked by sacrificial love. We are called to love God and to love others. We take part in the process of freeing one another to become the people we are called to be.

First, therefore, we are beings-in-relation. There is no other form of existence. Secondly, however, we are created and called to exist in a particular way—in a loving relationship with God and with one another. This has been corrupted and distorted by sin and by the sinful nature, so it is only through the destruction of sin on the cross that we are able to begin to live this new existence. In the first three chapters we explored the key to this: a life of intimate relationship with the Father, in Christ, and by the power of the Spirit. It is both Christ and the Spirit working in us, enabling us to love God and one another. It is our relationship with God the Father that gives us the security and affirmation we need to extend mercy and grace to others.

The only possible way of living out the Christian life is in relation to others. There is no such thing as a lone Christian, because once we are in relationship with God our identity becomes one of a person in relation to the whole people of God. We are related to the whole church. We are adopted into a new family; we are part of the people of God, the body of Christ, the bride of Christ, the temple, a holy priesthood, a royal nation. We do not possess this identity as individuals, but only collectively, and we are given this identity in order to be a witness to the character of God and the truth of Jesus in this world. The church is the salt and light of the world. Our identity as the people of God is given so that, together, we can represent him on this earth. Peter writes this, "But you are a chosen people, a royal priesthood, a holy nation, a people belonging to God, that you may declare the praises of him who called you out of darkness into his wonderful light. Once you were not a people, but now you are the people of God; once you had not received mercy, but now you have received mercy" (1 Pet :9–10). In this chapter, we will explore what it means to grow in our discipleship with one another. What does it mean to be a people who have received mercy, and how can we extend that mercy to one another and then out to the world?

SHAPED BY THE CROSS

There is a wealth of teaching in the Bible as to how we should behave towards one another. (I will not list all of the "one another" sayings in the Bible, but taking time to study and meditate on these exhortations, especially with others in our communities, is an amazingly fruitful way of exploring how we should love and respect one another, and what it means to be the people of God.) Jesus himself both taught about and modeled godly relationships. Paul, John, Peter, James, and the writer to the Hebrews all constantly exhort the people in their churches to behave towards one another in loving and self-giving ways. There are numerous references to the fact that God's people should be those who *love* each other, and to do this in tangible and recognizable ways. We are to forgive one another, submit to one another, to put one another first, to maintain unity, to serve one another, and to carry one another's burdens—at all costs. In the Old Testament, the book of Proverbs has countless sage aphorisms (or pithy sayings) on how to conduct our relationships, both with family and friends. Paul, in 1 Corinthians 13 describes the form of Christian love that we are to have for one another: not rude, boastful, unkind, envious, and self-seeking, but patient, forbearing, forgiving, truthful, protective, enduring. This kind of love keeps no record of wrongs, never accuses and is never spiteful. It is self-giving, encouraging, gracious, and generous. God has not left us wondering what these godly relationships might look like, but has spelled it out for us very clearly.

The most powerful example given to us of what this love looks like lies in the person of Jesus Christ, and his death on the cross. In John's Gospel, Jesus says this to his disciples, "A new command I give you: Love one another. As I have loved you, so you must love one another. By this all people will know that you are my disciples, if you love one another" (John 13:34–35). Later he says to them:

> As the Father has loved me, so have I loved you. Now remain in my love. If you obey my commands, you will remain in my love, just as I have obeyed my Father's commands and remain in his love. I have told you this so that my joy may be in you and that your joy may be complete. My command is this: Love each other as I have loved you. Greater love has no-one than this, that he lay down his life for his friends. (John 15:9–13)

We know what this *agape* love of Christ is, because we see it lived out both through Jesus's life on earth and his death. Furthermore, the only way we are able to achieve these Christlike relationships is because Christ now dwells in us through the Spirit, and because of the defeat of sin and death on the cross. Without the power of Christ in us, we would be unable to fulfill this one and only law. Galatians 6:2 says, "Bear one another's burdens, and thereby fulfill the law of Christ." Sometimes it is hard to absorb that there really are very few "rules" in the Christian life, but the reason for this is because there is one golden rule at the heart of everything, and actually keeping to this one "rule"—of loving one another, as Christ loves us—is both more testing and more fulfilling than keeping to a set of rules will ever be. If we think about it then, there is no possible way of becoming a disciple of Christ outside of relationships with others. The only way we can fulfill Christ's one law for his followers is to be with other followers, learning to love them as he has loved us (and as he also loves them).

There are, of course, those who may live in some form of isolation from others, whether literally in solitary confinement in prisons, or whether through a particular disability or incapacity which prevents relationships in the way we normally understand them. It is crucial, in these circumstances, that those who are not confined or prevented from relating to others, reach out and extend love to those who are. Christians are obliged to demonstrate the truth that all humanity is infinitely precious to God, especially to those on the fringes or edges of society, and to those who cannot return "love" in the way we understand it. The onus, then, is not on the isolated individual who is unable to reach out to others but on the church that can both ensure we are connected through prayer and through tangible forms of love, whether it is supporting the persecuted church and those in prison or spending time with those who are incapacitated in some way. We will discuss this in more detail below.

SHAPED BY OTHERS

All of us are affected and shaped by people, events, genetics, circumstances, and a whole host of other factors that determine our values, our preferences, our abilities, our opportunities, etc. We are not born as "free agents" in the sense we can do what we want, when we want, and where we want. As we have already discussed, there is so much about our lives that is actually beyond our control or influence, and is ultimately, only in God's hands. However, one of the crucial aspects of life that we can take responsibility for is how we conduct ourselves in our relationships. There is a saying, "You can choose your friends, but you can't choose your family." As Christians, this hits us as a double-whammy. We do not get to choose our blood family, and then we do not get to choose our church family. We are stuck both ways! It is in these real relationships that we are formed. Some of these relationships are healing and loving. Others are distant, and still others, antagonistic. Our relationships form us, and we form them. We are able to shape how they develop and the effect that they have on us. God in us and God with us has given us all the resources we need in Christ, the Word, and the Spirit to conduct Christlike relationships. In reality, however, it is an area in which most of us struggle. Maintaining loving relationships with our families, our church families, our friends, and our work colleagues is a real battle, but one in which we are called to persevere.

Most of us are acutely aware of the effect others have on us. We continuously have to react to others around us. Relationships vary. Some are good, but fleeting, or not necessarily of great import. Others have a lasting impact on us and can be powerfully and deeply transforming. Relationships can be both incredibly healing and unbelievably damaging. Family relationships are normally more intense than others, and can have a more enduring effect than others, but there are also other relationships that can be highly influential in molding the choices we make in life. These relationships include teachers, role models, mentors, our peers, and bosses (or anyone with any power or influence over us). All these relationships can affect and shape our choices, our values, our careers, where we live, and a whole host of other life-changing decisions. Other people matter to us, and we matter to them. We would not be who we are without the impact of other people on our lives. We are formed by the people who love us; we are formed by the people who hate us; we are formed by those we do not know, but know of; we are formed by people who have never noticed us; and by those who are closest to us. And in turn, we ourselves will be affecting those around us. How are we called to respond to this reality in a way that will form Christ in us, and help us form Christ in others?

YOU CAN CHOOSE YOUR FRIENDS. . .

Christians are saddled with two families: our church family and our blood family. It is in these families that we are most tested in our capacity to love as Christ loves. This is because it is in these relationships that we are denied the luxury of superficiality. It is so easy to be loving towards those we are never going to see again, because they will never know if we really live out our high claims to be self-sacrificing, serving, submissive, truthful, and forgiving. Our families know. They know when we are being hypocritical, mean, judgmental, lazy, proud, vindictive, dismissive, and the like. We are exposed by our families because they see us as we are. This is crucial in our journey of discipleship. If we are to grow truly into Christlikeness then integrity must be at the heart of it all. What we say *has* to align with how we behave. We cannot hide from one another. We must be known by others, and our words must match our deeds. It is imperative, therefore, that we have relationships where we are known, "warts an' all," because it is in those relationships that true transformation will be tested. In other relationships, we can become experts at pretence. I am always shocked at how well we human beings are able to deceive ourselves and one another, and sometimes for very long periods of time. The closer we are to one another, the harder it is to maintain our forms of deception. Jesus talks about becoming like little children in order to enter the kingdom of God. Willard comments on this in respect of our relationships, not just with God, but with one another.

> Interestingly, "growing up" is largely a matter of learning to hide our spirit behind our face, eyes, and language so that we can evade and manage others to achieve what we want and avoid what we fear. By contrast, the child's face is a constant epiphany because it doesn't yet know how to do this. It cannot manage its face. This is also true of adults in moments of great feeling—which is one reason why feeling is both greatly treasured and greatly feared. Those who have attained considerable spiritual stature are frequently noted for their "childlikeness." What this really means is that they do not use their face and body to hide their spiritual reality. In their body they are genuinely present to those around them. That is a great spiritual attainment or gift.[1]

We only know whether we have attained this integrity if we are with others with whom and from whom we cannot hide. Families are God's gift to us for this.

THE PROBLEM OF PARENTS

All of us have parents. They may be alive or dead. They may be together or separate. They may have brought us up or they may not. But all of us have parents, and our parents have a deep and lasting effect upon us. Philip Larkin, in his famous poem, had some insightful, if pessimistic, words to say about the effect parents have on their children in screwing them up! We may feel we agree with Larkin or we may feel our parents, or our parent, were the single most powerful source of blessing and love in our lives. However our parents have treated us, they will play an enormously important part in our formation, and learning how to respond to our parents (even after they are no longer with us) will be one of the most fundamental ways in which God forms Christlikeness in us. It is not insignificant that one of the Ten Commandments is to "honor your Father and your mother." If we come from families where both our parents were Christians, where they prayed for us and loved us unconditionally, where they worked for our

---

1. Willard, *The Divine Conspiracy*, 87.

good and our flourishing, where they affirmed us and empowered us, then the idea of honoring them will be not only natural but one of our greatest pleasures in life. As our parents gave to us, so we will desire to give back to them. Sadly, this tends to be an exception rather than a rule. Those kind of families are not the norm. If our parents have done their best, but actually, in many ways, have often hurt us or left us feeling damaged in some way, we will find it harder to honor them. First we have to face up the reality of how we feel about our parents. There will be no transformation until we can be perfectly honest. Through prayer, both on our own and with others, and the grace of forgiveness, we will find that, over time, we can release many of the hurts that have lodged in our hearts. Most of the people we encounter have relationships like these with their parents, where there are some real and genuine hurts that need to be forgiven and prayed through, but where there is also a basis for love and loyalty.

If however, we have had very traumatic childhoods, if our parents were absent or abusive or manipulative or cruel, the idea of honoring them and dealing with them in our lives may seem like an insurmountable struggle. What does honoring your parents mean if they have been terrible and destructive parents? Willard speaks of the importance of "pity" in family relationships. He uses this word, rather than "mercy" because it conveys God's gracious and patient forbearance with us. Jesus had compassion and pity on those who were suffering. God has pity on us as sinners. He forebears—he bears with us. It is only on this basis that we are able to forebear with one another. When we pity one another we bear with one another's faults and failings. For some of us we will only be able to reconcile our experiences as children when we are able to pity our parents, grandparents, and siblings in this sense; to extend mercy to them in a way that recognizes their failings and faults, and choosing to bear with them rather than storing up hatred and unforgiveness. Honoring our parents in certain circumstances may mean simply being thankful that they exist and respecting their role as "givers of life in the sequence of human existence."[2] As long as we are actually grateful for our existence, then, at the very least, we can be grateful to our parents that we exist and that they gave us life. From there, even if it takes years, we can pray for God's help to forgive them. If we believe in the power of God to transform, we can pray for the patience to pity them and to bear with them, rather than rejecting them completely. Obviously, in the

2. Ibid., 289.

case of abusive relationships, a strict distance must be maintained, but this does not prevent a community praying for the individuals concerned.

The same thing applies to our relationships with our siblings. Our siblings are people whom we can feel both intensely loyal to and deeply frustrated and angry with all at the same time. Over the years, in our ministry and in our own families, we have witnessed deep transformation in family relationships through prayer and through a determination to persevere in relationships. Forgiveness and repentance have been the key. Where there have been people praying and seeking the good of one another, we have seen both parental and sibling relationships utterly transformed and healed over time. The point about families is that we cannot really shake them off. We are held in them by our blood ties, and knowing this fact is one of the incentives to persevere in seeking healing and restoration. It can feel more costly at the time than walking away, but it is infinitely precious when healing comes. Church friendships are not just friendships any more; they are family relationships.

THE FAMILY OF GOD

Learning to persevere with our blood families equips us well for our church family. When we become Christians we get new parents, new siblings, and new children. For most of us, most of the time, this is a wonderful experience. Personally, I often thank God for the churches we have been privileged to be part of and for the new families God has given us in our years of ministry. They have been loving, giving, fun, prayerful, and kind. Both Nick and I and our children have experienced the depth and security of loving extended families, with adopted grannies, grandpas, parents, brothers, and sisters. Even in great churches, however, there are difficult relationships, and in some churches relationships can become horribly destructive. Any of us who have spent longer than a few months in a church will know that churches are sometimes the places of the bitterest disputes, the worst fallouts, and the most dysfunctional relationships. This can be the source of terrible disillusionment and pain, and can lead to people even abandoning church and never going back. There are analogies here with dysfunctional blood families, and (frustratingly sometimes) the calling upon us is not simply to walk away and never go back, but to learn how to forgive and release those who have hurt us.

When Peter comes to Jesus and asks him how many times he should forgive his brother when he sins against him, Jesus replies that he should forgive his brother, not seven times, but seventy times seven; in other words, endlessly. Jesus then tells him a story of a king who wants to settle accounts. This king initially decides to claim his debt from one of his servants by selling him and his wife and children to pay to the debt. As the servant pleads for his life, the king relents, and instead of selling the family, he cancels the debt. This same servant, having been set free, then goes out and finds another man who owes *him* some money. He grabs him violently and begins to choke him, ordering him to pay back what he owes. Like the first servant had just done, this fellow servant falls on his knees, begging him to be patient while he waits to pay his debt. The first servant refuses and has him thrown into prison. On hearing this, the king is incensed. He orders the servant to be imprisoned and tortured until he can pay what he owes. This story is called the parable of the Unmerciful Servant. It is a shocking parable of violence, imprisonment, and torture, and it is a graphic picture of what happens to human beings when they refuse to forgive and, instead, store up hatred and unforgiveness for one another. We become violent, imprisoned, and tortured in our souls. God has extended forgiveness and mercy to us. He has paid the price for our freedom. Repentance and forgiveness unlocks the door to the freedom offered and it is the key to freedom and healing for all involved.

Unfortunately, we have no excuses for refusing to forgive others. It is appalling to realize how many disputes and divisions there are in local congregations or between churches. Christian churches should be places where conflict resolution is practiced and modeled for everyone to see, but instead it sometimes seems we are particularly inept at handling conflict rather than excelling in it. As apprentices to Jesus, the process of working towards harmony and forgiveness in our relationships needs to be a priority. I would love to see the church take Jesus's teaching on reconciliation very, very seriously. Jesus said if we come to worship and we remember we are not reconciled to our brother or sister, then we should first go and make peace with them (Matt 5:23–24). It would be an extraordinary thing if, before we worshipped together, we ensured we were reconciled one to another. I imagine there would be an awful lot more honest conversations going on between us before we came to worship.

FORMED BY THE GOOD AND THE BAD

Having to live in communities that are like families to us is how we are formed by both the good and the bad: by those who love us, those who bless us, those who hurt us, and even those who hate us. We are formed in beautiful ways by those who love us. I am constantly amazed at the simplicity of the fact that a loving and affirming relationship can bring profound healing. When we know we are loved unconditionally and we are infinitely valued, we blossom and flourish. Relationships like these will have untold positive repercussions in our lives. If we are loved, we will then have the confidence and the security to love, encourage, and bless others. Loved people become loving people. We will achieve things we could never imagine. We will try new things and be more adventurous because we will not be fearful of failure. We will not be driven by fear of others or a desperate need for approval. We will handle rejection from others because we will know that fundamentally we are loved. We will not manipulate others to get the love we need because we will have it already. We will not bully or ridicule because we will be secure in who we are.

In the first few chapters we discussed how God is both *able* and *willing* to give us this deep sense of security and affirmation through the Son and the Spirit. For many of us, however, it takes years to absorb the reality and truth of this love. It is important, in this process, that we also learn to express this love to one another in tangible ways. I get frustrated when people teach or communicate that we should be fully and only satisfied by the presence and love of God. Is it really true that God is *all* we need? In one sense, yes, but in another sense, no. It sounds very holy and spiritual, but in reality we need the tangible and physical love and presence of one another as well, because God has made us dependent upon one another. He does not think it is good for human beings to be alone. Even Jesus had close friends with whom he was close and physically affectionate, both men and women. His will and purpose for us is that we should be able to love one another, as he loves us. If we lived in communities in which we demonstrated God's love to one another, we would be able to understand this love so much more and then, in turn, demonstrate love to those who still do not yet know him.

So we are formed and freed by those who love us, but we are also formed by those who irritate us and even those who hate us. Unfortunately, we live in imperfect communities where the truths about God are often distorted and our relationships with one another are marred by jealousy, control, gossip, dissension, and pride. However, these marred relationships also create opportunities for us to become more like Christ. Jesus himself was surrounded by difficult and testing relationships even among his friends, let alone his enemies! Graham Cooke, who has a teaching and prophetic ministry, tells the story of three men who for an extended period of time used to follow him around wherever he was speaking in order to campaign against him. Not only would they stand outside his events trying to persuade people not to enter, but they would then sit in the front row and heckle and distract him. Naturally, Graham Cooke's response to this was to plead with God to take them away and to deliver him from these three men whom he had nicknamed "the three stooges." They made life horribly difficult for him. After this had gone on for months, and he was praying about the situation yet again, he saw a picture of three men sculpting a huge slab of marble. As he watched, the three men worked away at the slab of marble, shaping it into a beautiful figure. He then felt God speak to him about the picture. The three stooges were all part of God's plan to shape and mold him. Even in their hatred and fear of him, and in their aggressive behavior, God was using these relationships to form Graham Cooke into something more beautiful. By having to live with them, and the frustration and difficulty they brought into his life, his character was being shaped and molded by God. He had to learn to bless those who were cursing him and to love those who hated him. Sometimes people call these difficult people in our lives "grace-growers" because we need to grow in grace towards them. It is salutary to remember that we too will be somebody's grace-grower!

PRACTICE MAKES PERFECT

People often observe that a person's true character is revealed in the choices a human being makes under pressure—the greater the pressure, the deeper the revelation, the truer the choice to the character's essential nature. Our ability to respond in Christlike ways is tested when other human beings put us under pressure, and we are tempted to be selfish, unkind, and unforgiving, instead of the opposite. One of the reasons we practice the holy habits is to help to train ourselves to respond well in the moments when we are under pressure. If we have spent time in God's presence in prayer, Bible study, meditating on Scripture, worship, fasting, silence, and the like, when we are faced with moments of pressure and we are tempted to behave in an ungodly way, we are much less likely to do so. Our characters are formed through our holy habits so that when they are tested in pressurized situations in our relationships we are more likely to respond well. Jonny Wilkinson, the English rugby player, used to spend hours and hours on his own, when he was younger, just kicking the ball. He did nothing else, just practiced kicking. When England was under pressure in the 2003 World Cup Final, with only twenty seconds to go in extra time, Wilkinson kicked the ball perfectly through the goal to win the match. His years and years of kicking paid off in a moment of pressure.

As we have already noted at various points, the Bible is actually very clear about how we should behave in our relationships, both towards God and towards one another. We have seen in the Sermon on the Mount that Jesus teaches about doing away with anger, lust, ridicule, and manipulation, and instead, becoming people who are quick to forgive, even our enemies. We are to speak lovingly and truthfully and refuse to use others as objects for our own benefit. We are to be people who never condemn others, who do not belittle, ridicule, or dismiss anyone. Jesus says, "You have heard that it was said to the people long ago, 'Do not murder, and anyone who does murder will be subject to judgement.' But I tell you that anyone who is angry with his brother will be subject to judgement. Again, anyone who says to his brother, 'Raca,' is answerable to the Sanhedrin. But anyone who says, 'You fool!' will be in danger of the fire of hell" (Matt 5:21–22). "Raca" is sometimes translated, "good-for-nothing" or "idiot." Other translations read, if you say, "I spit on you!" The translation "fool" definitely loses the bitterness and contempt in the original word. What Jesus is conveying is that when we treat others with contempt we are placing ourselves under the threat of serious judgment, because we are taking life from them. We are diminishing them. Astonishingly, he teaches that this is on a level with murder. One of the greatest challenges before us then is to resist treating anyone else, ever, with contempt, and thereby to judge them and to condemn them. Why is this?

To condemn something is to label it as fit for nothing. It has no purpose any more. It is useless and therefore worthless. When we condemn another this is what we are saying about them. This is the opposite of what God says about humanity. *No one* is useless. Everyone is of infinite worth and value. If we physically take another person's life, we have convinced ourselves that their lives are expendable, that they have no value. When we condemn a person, ridicule them, belittle them, and treat them as worthless, we are committing the same crime, in a different way. We are robbing them of their God-given worth. People who have been consistently condemned by others grow up with such a severely damaged self-image that it can take years of prayer and therapy to enable them to have healthy relationships. How do we change our perspective so that we restrain ourselves from condemning others?

The most effective way of breaking the habit of condemnation is to pray for people, and specifically, to pray for God's blessing upon them. This is the antidote that Jesus goes on to teach. "Love your enemies, and pray for those who persecute you, that you may be sons of your Father in heaven" (Matt 5:44). If we are prone to thinking that other people are "idiots," then praying for them will erode our disdainful attitudes towards them. Spending time asking God to bless those who we would love to judge and condemn is the only way that we are able to overcome our "murderous" thoughts and feelings towards them. It helps us to see them as God sees them and teaches us how much we too need God's mercy.

FORMED BY THE POOR

When Jesus allows the woman to anoint him with expensive ointment at Bethany, his disciples become overly pious and call it a waste of money. After all, the expensive ointment could have been sold and the money given to the poor. Jesus replies to them, "You will always have the poor with you, but you will not always have me." It is true, sadly, that the poor are always with us. Some of us would like to be able to forget the poor, but the Bible makes it abundantly clear that one of the marks of the people of God is that they should care for the poor. This is not an optional extra or something that only *some* Christians or *some* churches should be involved in. Just as we are commanded to love one another, so Jesus expects his followers to give to the needy. When Peter, James, and John agree to commission Paul and Barnabas to minister to the Gentiles, as they minister to the Jews, it is on one condition: that they continue to remember the poor—the very thing that Paul was eager to do (Gal 2:8–10).

I do not believe remembering the poor means just giving some of our money every now and then to worthy causes, although it is always good to give money. Working with the poor means spending time with people who have less than us, and seeking ways in which to give them back their dignity. If we ourselves are privileged in the sense that we have enough to live on, then we should be sharing what we have in different ways with those who do not have enough. There are countless ways in which we can do this and countless groups of people we could spend time with. It becomes something transforming for us when we see how actually it often just takes a tiny thing to make a difference. It is shocking sometimes to see how little effort it really takes to give the gift of recognizing another's worth. Anyone who has worked with prisoners, elderly people, disabled people, homeless people, excluded teenagers, will know that it is time spent with people, a smile, a touch, taking time to listen, that transforms a person's view of herself or himself. This is not to say that working with certain groups is not really costly, and those who work fulltime in these highly stressful environments certainly know this, but everyone acknowledges it is worth it for the moment of knowing a person has understood she or he matters and is truly valuable as a human being.

Spending time with those who have less than us is transforming for us as much, we hope, as it is for them. For us, it reminds us all the time to be grateful for what we have. It is a great way of ridding ourselves of greed and envy. Secondly, it keeps us humble. At one point, I coordinated a group of volunteers in a day center for the homeless in London. Some of our volunteers were people who had, at one time, been homeless themselves. Others were housewives, others retired people, and still others, people who were "important" at work. The business people used to come down early before work and spend an hour serving breakfast and washing dishes before heading off to the city. It made no difference to the people who used the day center who was who. Nobody knew and nobody cared. We were all equal in the task that we had chosen to do—to serve people who had been out on the street all night. The only thing the homeless people noticed, and what mattered to them, was how the people who served them treated them. A pastor once said to us, "Stay with the poor, because the poor don't massage your ego." Mother Theresa constantly spoke of the transforming effect of working and living with the poor. She said this, "Only in heaven will we see how much we owe to the poor for helping us to love God better because of them."

LIVING IN THE REAL WORLD

Working with the poor, or being poor ourselves, plunges us into very real, and very nitty gritty situations. This can be stressful and taxing, especially if it goes on day after day. Most of us have stress in our lives. Some of us experience enormously high levels of stress for extended periods. Living in difficult situations is oppressive and human beings often cannot bear too much reality. All of us have ways of escaping from reality and of living in fantasy worlds, and the worse our real situations are, the more we will be tempted to retreat into fantasy. It is crucial that we find ways of relaxing and activities that take us "out of ourselves," that give us a welcome break from the stresses and strains of life. Sport, leisure activities, good friendships, creative hobbies are all ways we unwind. There are some ways of escaping, however, that can be highly detrimental to our spiritual, mental, and emotional well-being and which then cause terrible damage to our relationships. In our culture, we are faced with multiple options of ways to escape into unreality. Fantasy can become a dangerous thing once it becomes obsessive, and can then impinge on our real lives in a way that can be genuinely destructive.

There tends to be a gender divide when it comes to certain pasttimes and the kind of activities that can become obsessions, although I would not want to press this point too much. Generally, men are more prone to becoming obsessed with video or computer games and women with the lives of others, but then I recently read an interesting article on the sharp rise among men in reading "chick-lit"! Gaming, however, is a huge issue for those of us in technologically advanced countries, as more of us spend hours in front of screens and involved in simulated lives. Anybody can become obsessed with games involving intrigue, violence, or sex. Similarly, pornography, romance, the lives of celebrities—all can become outlets for fantasy and obsession. The danger is that they have no connection with reality and with real relationships, and then reality becomes harder and harder to live with. We are plunged into worlds that become more real than our own worlds, and our relationships then suffer. Our relationships suffer on the most basic of levels because, like workaholics, we never have time for those around us. They also suffer because our chaotic, mundane, frustrating, real relationships will never match the unreal relationships we control on a screen, or in our heads. Life is not that exciting. We and our partners and friends will never be that glamorous, never that sexy, and never that rich. The more our fantasy worlds take over, the less time we will spend in our real, messy, less than perfect worlds.

Fantasy addictions to gaming, porn, and the internet have become serious problems for our society and are only going to get worse. There is currently much research being conducted on the effects of these kind of addictions on young people, but there is less and less of an age divide, and the real effects of this will not be known for some time. For the modern-day apprentice of Jesus Christ, it is something we have to take seriously. We need to keep our focus on what it means to live in the *real* world, in *real* relationships with *real* people, and to train ourselves and others in this. Firstly, we need to encourage one another to be honest about the escape routes that we have in life, and to examine how healthy they actually are. Further on, we will discuss the importance of confession. It is useless to take part in the practice of confession if we are not honest with ourselves and with others. Secondly, the holy habits of silence and solitude (isolating ourselves from screens and noise, and interaction with the world for periods of time) will be essential in breaking the power of involvement in unreal situations and fantasy.

If we are truly suffering from a real addiction, then others will need to commit to us in prayer for healing and release. We should expect to see more of these kinds of addictions in our churches in the years to come. Thirdly, we need to believe God is both willing and able to set us free from these behavior patterns. As we saw in chapter 4, desire is a powerful force in our lives, but the Spirit is able to transform our desires and to channel them away from destructive patterns and towards God. In chapter 2, I spoke of the kingdoms we inhabit and where we rule and reign—our places of influence. If we spend all our times in kingdoms that are, in fact, unreal, then all our energy, thoughts, emotions, and desires are channeled into what is, in fact, complete fiction. All our creative and life-giving energy is directed towards what is ultimately just narcissism, and is therefore wasted. Conversely, inhabiting the real world, in our thoughts, emotions, desires, etc., is the only possible way our lives can be used for the good of others.

LOVE, SEX, AND INTIMACY

Speaking of powerful desires, one of the great difficulties that we face as Christians in our society, and an issue that is linked to our tendency to relate to fantasy worlds, is the question of love, sex, and intimacy. How do we find expression for those three things in our relationships, and in our day-to-day lives? Human beings crave love and sex and intimacy, and the Bible teaches on all these things, but this does not mean that we are able to find easy ways in which to live with the teachings of Jesus. Like the question of suffering, we cannot just come up with one easy answer that will bring peace to our hearts and our minds for all time. Some people like to imagine that there really is an easy answer, and they even teach this in a simplistic fashion. It goes something like this, "Don't have any sexual relations until you get married, and then when you are married, never look at another man or woman in a lustful way." It is naïve, however, to think that these injunctions are either easy to live with, or being adhered to by the majority of men and women sitting in church. I have heard so many young people tell me that they are sick of hearing smug married women and men standing up and telling them "Just don't do it." Telling young people (or even older single people) not to have sex without (a) explaining properly *why* you think that, (b) acknowledging just how *difficult* that is to live out in our society, (c) offering ways of *supporting* those who would like to live a chaste or celibate lifestyle, and (d) being *honest* about the difficulties of sex within marriage instead of painting rosy pictures, is thoughtless and ineffective.

Because of the nature of our contemporary culture in the West, the question of love, sex, and intimacy is one of the central issues in contemporary discipleship for young people, and this is only a short section, but I will attempt to bring out what I see as some of the key principles. For a longer and more detailed treatment of this, I would highly recommend Lauren Winner's book, *Real Sex: The Naked Truth about Chastity,* which is the most sensible and realistic appraisal of the Christian attitude towards sex and relationships that I have read, and from which some of the principles that I outline will be drawn.

Firstly, however counter-cultural and difficult it is to live with, it seems that there are three lifestyles discussed in the Bible in relation to love and sex that are specifically *Christian*: marriage, chastity (no sex outside of marriage), and celibacy (a lifelong calling to live without a sexual relationship). In other words, following Jesus will entail conforming our relationships to one of these lifestyles. The Bible teaches that the context for sexual relationships is covenant. We have sex with those we are in covenant with, in the context of lifelong promises and commitment. The reason for this is that sex is not just a physical act, but has a spiritual dimension. Sex unites us with another person in an indissoluble bond, which is why it is supposed to be matched by an equally indissoluble bond in our hearts, our minds, and our spirits, and why this bond is declared publicly for all to see in a marriage ceremony. What we promise with our bodies to one another, we promise with our hearts. Otherwise, we are promising one thing with our bodies, uniting ourselves with another person, when in fact, we have no intention of uniting ourselves with them at all. When we become Christians, our bodies are no longer our own to do with them whatever we want. Paul writes that they now belong to the Lord, because we have been bought with a price (1 Cor 6:12–20). For this reason, we are to honor God with how we behave towards others, and to resist the temptation to promise one thing with our bodies, and to take another's body, but to withhold any emotional and spiritual commitment from them. Sex in the context of a covenant is much more likely to be healing for our whole beings than sex without commitments.

This message, that sex is given by God to be part of a covenant relationship is taught in different forms in many churches and, quite clearly, comes across in a contemporary Western society as utterly ludicrous to many, and totally naïve to others. Sex is no longer viewed as anything like this. It is for the most part never viewed as a spiritual act, or rather, an act with an inevitably spiritual dimension, as the Bible describes it. I would say that many older people still hold the view that sex should be something that happens between two people who love each other in some way, and that it should be an act of giving as well as taking. However, most people in our society would now think it entirely unrealistic to save sex for within a marriage. So the norm would be to have one sexual relationship after another in the context of a type of "commitment," but a commitment that actually could be broken by either party at a moment's notice. "Seeing someone," or even living with them has the semblance of commitment, but in reality, these are still fragile relationships at heart. Increasingly, however, sexual acts are becoming more and more divorced from even these fragile forms of commitment. Sex is not really just for the context of a loving relationship and is taking on a much more animalistic quality. Anyone who works with young people will know the levels of promiscuity and emotionless sex that people are engaged in, and that has now become the norm. It may not yet be totally acceptable across the board, but it is certainly accepted that people will regularly have sex with people they do not know, and will never see again, and that young men and women will not be "faithful" to their partners. Detached and disloyal sex is now normal.

THE "CHRISTIAN" RESPONSE?

In this context, many Christians are abandoning the traditional teaching on sex, marriage, and chastity on the grounds that it is just simply unrealistic and unreachable. Those Christians who wish to maintain the idea that sex should be expressed within lifelong, covenant relationships need to be aware of the fact that most people either disagree with them or find it simply impossible to live with. If we believe, however, that the Bible teaches this for good reasons, and because there is something in this teaching that will lead to healing and wholeness in relationships (because of the value that it places on another human being and on our bodies), we need to do three things. Firstly, we must teach on sex, love, and intimacy with honesty and integrity, and have good reasons for what we are saying. We cannot simply tell people not to "do it" without exploring the implications of chastity (both positive and negative) for young people today. We need to explain the concept of covenant and commitment, and why we believe this is the right context for sex, and to be realistic about the difficulties of conforming to that. Secondly, it is crucial we create forums where people can speak honestly about the real experiences real people have. There are so many lies told about sex by so many people. This does not help any of us. If we expect those in our families or those in our church to conform to certain standards, we must be *honest* about our own failings and weaknesses and help one another along the way. In reality, many more people live entirely without sex, and for much longer periods without sex, than we know or admit. Married people too can have difficult and damaging experiences of sex, or can be desperately lonely. Winner advocates much more openness on this topic in churches, and much more sharing of experiences between married and single people.

We must acknowledge that in order for people to be either chaste, celibate, or faithful to partners in marriage, they need the support, affection, and love of a community. I cannot bear it when people tell me they are lonely, or have been lonely, in a church. A church is the last place we should feel lonely, and yet it happens. With the breakdown of family life and communities, loneliness is one of the deepest problems in our society. Many, many people suffer from low self-esteem and depression. In those situations, it is natural to turn to sexual relationships for love and intimacy and a sense of self-worth. We all crave love, intimacy, and sex, and it is natural to equate all three, but in reality, it is easy to have sex without love and intimacy, and doing this can sometimes just make the loneliness worse. If we live in communities where there is love and intimacy, we are far more likely to be able to live without sex. Too often, churches are legalistic about sex without acknowledging that everyone should be taking part in loving and welcoming and caring for one another. We cannot just lay burdens on people that are too hard to carry, and then reject them when they cannot carry them. Learning to live a chaste life outside marriage, or a faithful life within a marriage can be almost impossible if we are struggling with issues of self-esteem, self-worth, and rejection. We cannot just leave people on their own to work all these things out. We need to provide loving, caring, nurturing, and affectionate communities where we can learn about the security, value, and love God offers us in Christ. Furthermore, we need to learn to be patient and honest with one another on this journey.

FRIENDS

One of the reasons I believe chastity and celibacy should not be rejected as Christian lifestyles, even if they are hard to live with, is because of the lives of those I see who have chosen to live in this way. We have heard so many stories of people who have come to the point in their lives, either at a young age or after a number of relationships, when they have decided that unless or until they are married, then they will not have sex with another person. They do this on the grounds that they believe that this is what it means to follow Jesus. In doing this, they are not claiming it is easy, or even very fun sometimes, to be different and to stand out among their peers. It is not easy to live with ridicule, scorn, sexual frustration, or loneliness. There are genuinely negative and positive aspects to chastity. It is costly, just as it can be costly to stay faithful to a husband or wife in a difficult marriage. However, following Jesus's teachings in relationships is the grounds for a new type of freedom. Those who choose these lifestyles have a freedom in their spiritual lives, and actually, a much greater freedom in their friendships. If we know that we have made a decision not to allow our good friendships to become sexual relationships unless we are prepared to make a lifelong promise to that person, then our friendships are not diminished by that but are deeper and longer lasting. Friendships without the possibility of sex are hugely underrated and undervalued in our society. We can turn on the television at any time, watch any contemporary film, and the idea that friends should have sex if they suddenly find they are attracted to each other is commonplace. We are encouraged to follow our every sexual desire, regardless of how long they may last, and regardless of the consequences. Why say no? This message is based on a terribly distorted account of relationships, completely ignoring the real life consequences of a relationship that goes from friendship to sex. People are not left unchanged, and relationships do not stay the same. New dimensions of jealousy, insecurity, and heightened emotion creep in, and other friendships are affected. Chaste friendships are totally different from this. They are much more secure, more healing, and give us far more dignity than casual or fragile sexual relationships. It is possible for a relationship to be more empowering, more releasing, and even more intimate without sex than it is with sex. If we wish to live chaste or celibate lifestyles then deep, honest, and affectionate relationships with both men and women will be one of the ways that we will be empowered to do this. As communities, we must acknowledge the support that we all need from one another to live radically counter-cultural lifestyles.

THE PROBLEM OF SIN

One of the difficulties for Christians, is that what we label as "immoral" ways of behaving often just do not seem to have immediate or terrible consequences. Sometimes this is because what people in church label as "sin" is particularly petty and silly. With other forms of "sinful" behavior, it may be that it is just not that obvious at the time. For example, it is quite clear that not all sexual relationships outside of marriage are "bad" relationships. Many couples have loving, giving, and generous relationships and the fact that they are having sex just seems to bring them closer. How do we reconcile teaching on marriage, celibacy, and chastity with the obvious goodness of some relationships around us, and that the fact that some of the people having sex outside of marriage seem perfectly free and happy? Other things like "white lies," recreational drugs, or the occasional porn video, do not seem to be overtly harmful. It is important to acknowledge the reality of this, and not to try and convince young Christians that all immorality leads to immediate and lasting misery. It simply does not. Sin can often seem not really very "sinful." Importantly, however, the question for the apprentice of Jesus is not actually about our short-term happiness or fulfilling our every desire but about whether what we are doing is genuinely loving to God and genuinely loving and freeing to those around us. What we do in our bodies and with our bodies has eternal significance. It shapes and molds who we are, and affects those around us. We are all of us "never-ceasing spiritual beings with a unique eternal calling to count for good in God's great universe." Certain patterns of behavior may seem "fun" or "harmless" for a while, but if we become accustomed to fulfilling our own desires before the desires of others, to taking promises lightly or refusing to give our bodies the worth that God gives to them (as the place in which he dwells), in the long term our relationship with God and with others will slowly diminish. The fact that Jesus had to die to deliver us from sin shows us how seriously God takes sin, how truly destructive it can be, and how much we, as forgiven and released sinners, should make every effort to sow to the Spirit rather than the sinful nature. This is true freedom.

CONFESSION

In a previous chapter, I touched briefly on the practice of confession, of speaking truthfully to another about the state of our hearts and minds. In whatever form we practice it, confession of sin should be a part of our corporate life together. James links the confession of sin to healing: "Therefore, confess your sins to one another and pray for one another, that you may be healed" (Jas 5:16). John writes, "If we say we have no sin, we deceive ourselves, and the truth is not in us. If we confess our sins, he is faithful and just to forgive us our sins and to cleanse us from all unrighteousness" (1 John 1:8–9). The idea that we can actually do *anything* in isolation is not really a Christian idea. Christians belong to the body of Christ, and so what we do, affects others. We are responsible for others and we are responsible to others. How we behave, therefore, is a matter that affects everybody, and not just ourselves. Behavior that is damaging to ourselves or to others is something that has repercussions for whole communities, and is no longer a private affair. We see this clearly in blood families, and we see it clearly in church families. Confession and repentance is a powerful way of resisting the effects of sin.

The Bible has a number of words and concepts for "sin." It is variously described as ungodliness, perversion, rebellion, missing the mark, falling short, a debt, a transgression, turning one's ear away, and a lack of righteousness. Sin is both a state (something we are enslaved to) and acts (things we do that are contrary to God's will). Sin is when I put myself and my concerns before God or when I place myself at the center of my world, ignoring God and others. But sin is not just an individual problem. Sin has devastating effects on families, friendships, and communities. This is why we are exhorted over and over again in the Bible to be quick to repent of our sins, to turn away from our self-centeredness and to become God-centered, so that we allow God to stem the destruction that sin causes. Psalm 32 is a description of a person's experience of confession, and receiving forgiveness from God.

> Blessed is he whose transgressions are forgiven, whose sins are covered. Blessed is the man whose sin the Lord does not count against him and in whose spirit there is no deceit. While I kept silence, my bones wasted away through my groaning all day long. For day and night your hand was heavy upon me; my strength was sapped as in the heat of summer. Then I acknowledged my sin to you, and did not cover up my iniquity. I said, "I will confess my transgressions to the Lord"—and you forgave the guilt of my sin. Therefore let everyone who is godly pray to you while you may be found; surely when the mighty waters rise, they will not reach him. You are my hiding place; you will protect me from trouble and surround me with songs of deliverance. I will instruct you and teach you in the way you should go; I will counsel you and watch over you. Do not be like the horse or the mule, which have no understanding but must be controlled by bit and bridle or they will not come to you. Many are the woes of the wicked, but the Lord's unfailing love surrounds the man who trust in him. Rejoice in the Lord and be glad you righteous; sing, all you who are upright in heart.

The psalmist is inwardly suffering both mentally and physically as a result of unconfessed sin. His body is wasting away with the stress and strain of not acknowledging his sin to God, and he feels as if he is in a spiritual desert. His confession brings the knowledge of forgiveness, great relief, freedom, and joy. He is no longer overwhelmed, but conscious of God's great mercy and deliverance. The Lord speaks to him, promising his counsel and his guidance, and warning him not to be stubborn, angry, or hard-hearted. The upright in heart are not those who never do anything wrong, because we all do wrong things all the time. The upright in heart are those who are quick to confess and repent. Our intimate friendships are those in which we are able to practice confession. It is in relationships of love and trust that we can receive healing from one another by speaking truthfully about what we are struggling with and why, and in that context to receive forgiveness and restoration. This will bring enormous freedom both in our relationship with God and with one another.

The Disciple

APPRENTICES TO MASTER ARTISANS

Learning to be more Christlike in our relationships is not something that we discover in isolation. We can only test our level of competence, as it were, in concrete relationships with the people around us. It is not something that we can achieve in theory, only in practice. Many of us have had the privilege of having this modeled and nurtured in our lives by others. Others of us have had to muddle along, and despite bad role models, have done the best we can. It helps if we see something put into practice in the lives of others, just as it helps if we are given a head-start in life by a particular upbringing. If you have ever learned anything on your own, you will know the enormous difference between self-taught skills and ones that you are taught by others. Most of us, by adulthood, will have learned a good number of things on our own. However, if we have ever been taught or mentored by anyone—whether that was a good teacher, a sports coach, or a mentor—we will know the difference. Being coached by another who is wiser and more able than we are is amazing. Not only does it succeed in the impartation of skills, but it also gives us the opportunity to learn about potential pitfalls, to glean from another's wisdom, and to gain confidence. It is invaluable in the learning of new skills. The power of impartation in the Christian life cannot be underestimated, and is one of the great strengths of being part of a community. Faith, wisdom, love, and holiness are all "catching" or contagious. The more we hang around people who are living Christlike lives, the more we will learn what that means. We are affected by others, and we in turn, affect others, both positively and negatively. Our goal should be to impart good things to those around us and to be a transforming force for good. We are responsible for others and to others. What we do with our bodies matters. What we do with our time and our minds matters. It is not just a question of my own pursuit of holiness or my failure to pursue holiness but it is a question of the impact that I have on others around me. I can wound or I can heal. I can bless or I can curse. I can nurture or I can condemn.

I began this book by speaking of the Christian life as one of apprenticeship. I would love to see many, many more women and men involved in taking on apprentices. There are some great discipleship movements going on around the world, but there are also huge gaps. I find this especially true for women, as traditionally men have done all the discipling, and they very naturally, choose to disciple other men. Women are falling through the gap somewhat, but this is not a matter for discouragement. Women must simply begin to take part in the process of nurturing others, and things will begin to change. As I said in the beginning, apprenticeship is better done through relationships rather than programs and is more effective in smaller rather than larger groups, or even one to one. Finding a master artisan is a gift, and many of us never actually have one person who takes us under her wing, but this does not mean that we cannot take part in the community process of encouraging one another to grow in our apprenticeship of Jesus. In the final chapter, I will specifically address the question of mentoring, as I see this as a crucial practice for the church in the making of disciples.

WHERE THE SPIRIT OF THE LORD IS. . .

The church is the community of Christ and the Spirit, and it is impossible to love one another without the presence of God. It is his presence that transforms us so that we can even contemplate leaving our old selfish ways behind, and begin to love and free one another. When we live in church families, it is not all about what the family or the community can do for me, but what I can do for others. When this works well it can have untold blessings in people's lives, spilling out into the world. Communities that learn how to love truthfully, generously, and self-sacrificially will be infinitely attractive to those on the outside. Moreover, we will not be able to help ourselves from wanting to extend this love to others in welcome. If we are a people who know the mercy that we have received, we will then be able to extend this to others. I love the verses in Romans 12 as a picture of a Christian community and for years I have aspired to be part of a community that understands what it means to put these verses into practice. Instead of listing holy habits at the end of this chapter, I have chosen to finish with the words of Paul.

> Love must be sincere. Hate what is evil; cling to what is good. Be devoted to one another in brotherly and sisterly love. Honor one another above yourselves. Never be lacking in zeal, but keep your spiritual fervor, serving the Lord. Be joyful in hope, patient in affliction, faithful in prayer. Share with God's people who are in need. Practice hospitality. Bless those who persecute you; bless and do not curse. Rejoice with those who rejoice; mourn with those who mourn. Live in harmony with one another. Do not be proud, but be willing to associate with people of low position. Do not be conceited. Do not repay anyone evil for evil. Be careful to do what is right in the eyes of everybody. If it is possible, as far as it depends on you, live at peace with everyone. Do not take revenge,

my friends, but leave room for God's wrath, for it is written: "It is mine to avenge: I will repay," says the Lord. On the contrary,

"If your enemy is hungry, feed him;
if he is thirsty, give him something to drink.
In doing this, you will heap burning coals on his head."
Do not overcome by evil, but overcome evil with good.
(Rom 12:9–21)

seven

Formed to Give Away

MENTORING OTHERS

I BEGAN THIS BOOK by considering the fact that there is a perceived "crisis" in discipleship in the Western church. I do not particularly think this is something the church was once good at and is now bad at. It is probably more the case that we are at a stage in history, and in our culture, where we are beginning to see the value of discipling more and more, and thus notice the lack of it when it is not there. There should always be those who call us back to the Great Commission, reminding us that the call upon the Christian is to become a disciple of Jesus, so that she or he, in turn, can make disciples. What we are realizing afresh is that this process is not one that just "happens" around us. It is a process we must engage in actively and intentionally. Being formed as apprentices to Jesus happens in the dynamic of engaging in the gracious work of the Son and the Spirit in our lives, calling us into a deeper love and a greater obedience of the Father. We cannot do this on our own, or by ourselves, and God gives us one another as gifts on this journey.

I wish to conclude, in this penultimate chapter, by changing tack a little bit and exploring some of the principles and practices of mentoring, as the idea of mentoring one another is at the heart of apprenticeship. Jesus's disciples learned because they were simply "with him." They lived their day-to-day lives in his company. They listened to him teach the crowds, they watched him pray, they saw him heal others, they asked him to explain what he meant when they were confused, they ate with him, walked with him, questioned him, laughed with him, and cried with him. Jesus and his followers genuinely loved each other, and engaged with each other in deep and real ways. In the Christian life, we are all first followers of Jesus, and we learn from him. Primarily, it is God who shapes and forms us, but we also learn from one another.

There are so many ways of being apprentices of one another that I am hesitant about being too precise about the practicalities of mentoring. For example, I have noticed that men and women go about mentoring very differently, both as those who act as mentors and what they want from a mentoring relationship. It is also clear that different age groups respond to different forms of teaching, or ways of relating and communicating. What is useful for one person may be useless for another. For this reason, I will not focus on *how* we might take part in the mentoring of others, but more *why* this might be a fruitful part of the Christian life. Mostly, in this chapter, I am speaking about relationships of one Christian with another, where one person has something to impart and the other has something to learn, and I am thinking about this in the context of relationships of either one to one or small groups where this is acknowledged. This happens all the time in the workplace. We consciously and intentionally learn from others. Mentoring others in a church setting is a very personal thing, and it is shaped by our personalities and the personalities of those whom we mentor. The following are some of my personal insights, but because of the particular nature of mentoring these may not be applicable to everyone. However, I hope I manage to draw out some principles that may be useful for others in different situations. The practicalities can then be worked out and adjusted depending on the particularities of any given situation and relationship.

BECOMING A PARENT

At one point in our ministry, Nick and I found ourselves working exclusively with university students, which was a new thing for both of us. We were a bit disconcerted, however, when they immediately cast us in the role of "father" and "mother." At first, I was quite uncomfortable with this, and wondered if it was healthy. Did it signal too much dependence? Was it actually unhelpful? After all, we *were* parents, to our own boys, and maybe we should think of another way of relating to the young people in our church.

It was not a role I was looking for or that I wanted to be stuck with. However, the image did stick, and after a while, I began to see that it was not all negative, and that there is something generative and right about the idea of pastors as parents, as long as it is handled well. I am very aware of all of the pitfalls of using a "parenting" image, but despite the problems, I have come to think that there is also something in the image of parenting that is amazingly fruitful for the concept of discipleship and mission, again, if it is framed, articulated, and lived out well. I began to reflect on the concept of parenting as an analogy for discipleship and mission, and have become convinced that it is useful in many ways.

Although in this case, we *were* actually old enough to be their parents, by using the term "parenting" I do not mean to communicate that this is age-related. I am not really talking about relationships of one person who is twenty years older than another, but a variety of relationships and ages, where one person plays a spiritually parental role in another person's life. I hope it will become clear that I mean this to be a freeing and a fluid role, and not something that exists within a static, hierarchical structure. Spiritual "fathers" and "mothers" can be people who are chronologically young themselves, and people who are not much older than those who they are mentoring. Paul calls Timothy his "son" but also appoints him to instruct and teach others. He encourages Timothy not to be intimidated by the fact that he is young and will have to instruct those who are older than him. "Don't let anyone look down on you because you are young, but set an example for the believers in speech, in life, in love, in faith, in purity" (1 Tim 4:12). Youth is not a barrier to becoming a mentor and an example for others. I have often been inspired and instructed by those who are younger than me. Moreover, I do not have in mind any particularly prescribed roles for mothers and fathers. I believe men and women often bring different gifts in teaching, training, and nurturing others, but many men have nurturing traits normally associated with women, and women can take up roles normally associated with men. If possible, throughout the Christian life, we should be mentored by both men and women. Timothy was first trained and instructed in the faith by his mother and grandmother. He then came under Paul's wing and was encouraged and trained by him. Of course we should be sensitive to the potentially intense nature of one-to-one mentoring, and not be foolish about intense and private relationships with the opposite sex, but unless there are good reasons to keep our distance, it is perfectly right and proper for both men and women to work in mixed groups with either a man or a woman.

PARENTING AND THE GOSPEL

The notion of parenting and parenthood is at the heart of the gospel. Jesus came to earth to call humanity back to the Father, and God acts and relates to us, not only as our father, but as our mother. God is our perfect parent. We find our true identity when we understand that we are his children, that we are adopted into a new family, with God as our father and our mother, and Jesus as our brother, in whom we are all brothers and sisters. As we have been discussing throughout the book, the metaphor of the family is so strong for Christians, that it is inescapable. We all relate to God as our Father, and sometimes as our mother, and throughout the Old and New Testaments, the Bible is littered with parental images of God. He loves us unconditionally, he nurtures us, he protects us, he disciplines us, he gives good gifts to us, and much more. In the church, we are all fathers, mothers, sisters, brothers, and children. Moreover, the Christian life is about pro-creation and new birth. Jesus described the process of putting our faith in him as being "born again" (John 3:5–8). The Spirit gives new life and new creation to us. We become people who are recreated by God in his Son through the power of the Spirit (2 Cor 5:17). We are Jesus's children and brothers and sisters at the same time (Heb 2).

Paul, the greatest missionary and maker of disciples, also cast himself in the role of a parent. He uses powerful parental imagery, both maternal and paternal, to describe his relationship with those under his spiritual care. "As apostles of Christ we could have been a burden to you, but we were gentle among you, like a mother caring for her little children" (1 Thess 2:7). "My dear children, for whom I am again in the pains of childbirth until Christ is formed in you, how I wish I could be with you now and change my tone, because I am perplexed about you" (Gal 4:19–20). And as we have seen, Timothy is Paul's spiritual "son." The making of disciples entails a mothering and a fathering role. Moreover, there is something basic in the concept of parenting in respect of discipling, evangelism, mission, and the spread of the gospel. The work of the kingdom begins with the nurturing of disciples. Throughout church history, representatives of Christ have taken on parental roles in the church. Priests are sometimes called, "Father," the Abbot of a monastery has a paternal role, the Abbess is the "Mother Superior." This has the potential for a positive or a negative impact.

Some parenting can be enabling, empowering, equipping, and releasing. Other parenting can be stifling, abusive, infantilizing, and repressive. The church has excelled at both.

When we were cast as parents, it posed a challenge for us. We were not going to change it without (ironically) becoming authoritarian about the use of words, so how could we learn to be good parents and not bad ones. Everyone knows that there are good and bad parents. We can still love our parents if they are bad ones. We can still be deeply bonded to our parents, even if they hurt us, reject us, and manipulate us, but the effect of a bad parent will last a lifetime. Bad parenting handicaps us, leaves us with scars that need to be healed and pain that can damage others—psychological, emotional, and even physical damage. Anyone who has had a damaging parent or parental figure knows this. This is why the abuse or manipulation carried out by some church leaders is so serious; because it is a gross distortion of a relationship of trust that is akin to a parental relationship, and the damage can last a lifetime.

Good parents, in contrast, are enablers: those who build up, who promote health, who generate life, who establish strong foundations, who form us for a good life with healthy relationships and the ability to be a blessing to others. Most important, good parents are parents who let go of their children to see them flourish and grow in their own right and in their own spheres. Good parents are prepared to sacrifice their own well-being, comforts, achievements, and much more for the sake of their children. They want to see the next generation flourish and blossom, to go far beyond what they themselves were able to do. Our desire as Christians should be to strengthen and equip those who are with us, so that they flourish as disciples—to love them in ways that will form Christ in them. We want to encourage one another to love and follow Jesus in all and every circumstance, so that they are set free from us, and so that they are equipped for the whole of life.

PARENTS, APPRENTICES, AND MISSION

The natural world often helps us think theologically. Jesus illustrated truths about the kingdom of God from the world around him: seeds, plants, yeast, babies being born. The world of family life gives us a way of understanding the spiritual life. Human beings function in families. In fact, there is no other way to be a human being, other than being created by other human beings, and then being dependent upon them. A "family" is the context in which this is lived out. Even in places where children no longer live in their own families, society seeks to place people in something approximating to family life. It is generally acknowledged that this is the healthiest and best context for a human being to thrive. Families may function or dis-function, but, despite even the most liberal of agendas, most will agree that a healthy family-type community is the very best for human flourishing, and so I use the term "family" in the broad, extended sense. I have taken a few principles from a model of good parenting in order to apply that to the spiritual task of making disciples, who will, in turn, go on to make other disciples, and to form new communities or churches. In other words, this is relevant for both discipleship and mission. These principles, like all analogies, are not perfect. There will be gaps and there will be some aspects that work better than others. It is, however, simply a framework to help us in our thinking and our practice of what it is we are doing when we are attempting to form communities that are focused on both discipleship and sending, and seeking to form each other in Christlikeness. If we are aiming to be "good" parents, what exactly are we aiming for?

Good Parents:

a) prepare their children to leave home;
b) adapt to the different phases of a child growing up;
c) strike a balance between control and freedom;
d) prepare children to take responsibility, to make good decisions of their own, and to form healthy relationships;
e) give children the freedom to fail;
f) delight in their children's differences (from themselves and from their siblings);
g) impart values by teaching them *and* modeling them;
h) act as guides and friends throughout a child's life; and
i) depend on their grown up children when they need to exercise humility and model teachability.

Grown up Children:

a) will form households and families of their own that have their own distinctive culture;
b) will retain the some of the values of their parents; and
c) will also be formed by influences outside the family.

PREPARING TO LEAVE HOME

Firstly, good parents prepare their children to leave home. Despite the growing number of adult children who are forced to stay in the parental home for economic reasons, we all have a sense at a certain moment in our adult lives that we should leave our parental home. This often coincides with a similar sentiment in our parents—possibly when they have become fed up of clearing up after a 25 year old! It is right to leave home, to fly the nest, to find a place of our own. Church leaders can be very possessive of the people in their church, but this is neither good for discipleship nor for mission. Ministers and pastors are often tempted to hold on to their "good" people. They feel that they have invested so much, loved, trained, given, nurtured, and now they want to see some return for the investment. If we are part of a church tradition that measures "success" in numerical growth, this puts enormous pressure on pastors or ministers to grow their own particular church in terms of "bums on seats." This, however, does not make for good practice in discipling others.

Churches that have a strong emphasis on discipleship and mission will invest *in order to send out*. Missional churches will put a much greater emphasis on people "growing up" and leaving home than on staying at home at all costs. Ironically, therefore, a church that is "successful" in mission and church planting may not be one that is always growing numerically, because it will be a church that is always sending out its best, always releasing people to go and to make disciples. This may not always mean "leaving" the church. It may mean branching out in a new way, starting a new project, doing something differently from how we have been taught. There is a way of making a healthy break from our parents that is good for us and good for them. Even when our children are young, part of our job is to begin to equip them to leave, to live life without us, to anticipate, and to look forward to independence. Tempting as it may be to hold on to people, and to want to keep them to ourselves to grow "our" church, if we are truly focused on discipleship and mission, we will be prepared to let people go. The gathering and keeping mentality that goes on in many churches can become unhealthy, tie people down when they are ready for adventure, independence, and new tasks, and prevent people from "growing up."

ADAPTING TO GROWING CHILDREN

Good parents adapt to the different phases of their children as they grow up. Children grow, and as they grow, they change, and, as they change, parents need to adapt their responses to their children. It would be entirely inappropriate to treat a sixteen year old like a four year old. The New Testament has numerous references to discipleship as the process of "growing up" and maturing. Paul, Peter, and the writer of Hebrews all use parental imagery and food imagery in relation to discipleship. The young in the faith are to be fed on baby-milk. Those who are more mature are ready for solid food. We have different phases of growing up. Those who are not ready should not be given great responsibilities. It is not fair to them or to others. Church communities should be adaptable to the different stages of growing up, and be alert to when people are ready for the next stage. If a person is a grown up, we must stop treating her or him like a child. We must provide them with solid food, and release them to become leaders and teachers of others. If we fail to do this, we will have congregations of bored and frustrated people, and eventually we will lose them. My experience of working with young people is that they are ready for leadership much earlier than we think they are. In many cultures, children as young as seven or eight care for younger siblings or cousins. They take on a parental role, and when given this responsibility, they do it well, guarding the toddlers from the fire, feeding them, changing diapers, etc. Most people grow into the responsibilities that they are given.

LETTING GO TO THE SPIRIT

Thirdly, good parents strike a balance between control and freedom. I have been shocked over the years by how controlling some church leaders are, even over adults, not just over the youth. Jesus never controlled people, and warns us strongly against manipulation (Matt 5:37). Of course, when children are young, they need supervision and control. Adults carefully control the environment that little children live in so as to protect them from harm. It would be irresponsible to do anything else. The protective instinct, however, can sometimes become stifling, if it is exercised in the wrong way or at the wrong age. Years ago we heard some parenting talks, advocating teaching children to make their own decisions from the age of eight, in order that they should be equipped to make all their own decisions, more or less, by the age of twelve. This does not mean we abandon them at the age of twelve, but simply that we trust them at a young age to start to make decisions for themselves. In our society we have a strange attitude to our children. On the one hand, we are terribly over-protective and risk averse when it comes to potential physical danger. On the other hand, we allow them to be exposed to terrible images through films and games and the like, which are shaping who they are in profound ways. I often feel we should exercise more control in the latter and less control in the former.

When we lived in Sheffield, we spent some time with friends at St. Thomas, Crookes. Under the leadership of Mike Breen, St. Thomas's talked of a culture of "low control," specifically as a way of releasing the dynamic of mission and evangelism. This appealed to us enormously. It struck us as being right and healthy. We had always operated on this basis, but had never articulated it as such. Later, I read Roland Allen's books on mission in China where he advocates exactly the same thing, except that his perspective is more intentionally and overtly focused on the work of the Spirit. Allen placed a high value on the control of the Spirit in churches in matters of ethics, discipleship, church leadership, and mission. He writes:

> It is not easy for us today so to trust the Holy Ghost. We can more easily believe in His work in us and through us, than we can believe in His work in and through our converts: we cannot trust our converts to Him. But that is one of the most obvious lessons which the study of St. Paul's work teaches us. I believe that we have still much to learn from his example.[1]

Allen urges leaders to train their "converts" to be independent from them and to learn to rely on the leading of the Spirit for themselves. A failure to do so results in passive followers, who do not understand that it is every disciple's task to preach the gospel.[2] Low control can be counterintuitive, especially if we are naturally controlling people, but interest and investment in children, rather than control, is what prepares them for responsibility, decision-making, and healthy relationships. This is at the heart of letting people go to become and to make disciples, and to take the initiative in mission. Another great missionary, who has written one of my favorite books on missionary work, is Vincent Donovan. On the practice of making disciples so that they in turn become those who make disciples, he writes:

1. Allen, *Missionary Methods*, vii.
2. Ibid., 81–82.

> They too can learn to take steps necessary to becoming a mission-
> ary people, with their own heralds of the gospel, a people overcome
> with the consuming conviction of Paul that it will be "woe to them
> if they do not preach the gospel." Step by painful step. And the last
> step the most painful of all, the step leading to the conclusion that
> the whole process is really out of one's control after all; that there is
> a Spirit moving through the world and through Africa, and what
> control there is lies with that Spirit.[3]

Investment in the "early years," or in the first couple of years, of a person
becoming a Christian, should give way to the handing over of responsibility, to empowerment, to trust. We must acknowledge a person's right to
make their own decisions how and when they see fit. The church leader's
job is not to run other people's lives, but rather to equip them to run their
own and, in turn, to nurture others. This can start from a very early age.

FREEDOM TO FAIL

Fourthly, good parents give their children the freedom to fail. One of the
things that all parents notice about other parents is how pushy they are!
The problem for parents is that we try to live out our lives through our
children, expecting them to succeed where we perhaps failed, and believing
that their achievements reflect well on us. Their successes vindicate us and
validate us as parents. The problem with this mentality is that the converse
will also be true. Their failures will be our failure, and we will be unable to
cope with anything that makes us look bad or feel as if we ourselves have
failed. It is not good for us, and certainly not good for our children to function in this way. We cannot rely on our children's successes to make us feel
better or look good. If we do, we will never release them properly to become
themselves. So many of us are caught in the cycle of endlessly seeking parental approval (sometimes even into our old age) and we become scared
of failure, so we take very few risks. If we do fail, it becomes a catastrophic
event, rather than something we can learn from, pick ourselves up from
and move on. It is only when we are set free to fail that we really learn and
grow into adulthood. The freedom to fail is essential in an apprenticeship.
I am amazed at how much pressure there is on children in some Christian
families to be perfect. We never apply those standards to ourselves, why on
earth do we think we can apply them to our children?

3. Donovan, *Christianity Rediscovered*, 180.

Of course, as responsible adults in any given situation, we feel the burden to prevent others from taking foolish risks. Many people get badly hurt or damaged through foolish decisions. Parents play an important role in guarding and imparting wisdom and are sometimes wiser than we would like to think they are. I love one of the quotes that is attributed to Mark Twain. It has such a ring of truth about it. "When I was a boy of fourteen, my father was so ignorant I could hardly stand to have the old man around. But when I got to be twenty-one, I was astonished by how much he'd learned in seven years." Being given the privilege of mentoring others, however, does not mean that we run their lives. There are many, many times that Nick and I, as pastors, have seen people making decisions that are sometimes unwise and risky, sometimes plain stupid, and sometimes disastrous. We too have made our fair share of stupid and unwise decisions in our lives. There are things we deeply regret, and we have been grateful for friends and mentors who have advised us along the way, and kept us from even worse decisions, or who have helped us out of messes that we have created. We cannot however, control other people, or order them to obey us. This is to maintain human beings in childishness and disempowerment. It will not lead to a free and joyful following of Jesus Christ and is not how God himself treats us. We can offer what little wisdom we have, but we must allow others to explore, and at times, to make mistakes. This is how we learn, and how they will too.

In some churches, there is a great emphasis on the "authority" of the leader. Leaders see it as their job to correct and to discipline others, and the congregation is expected to submit to the decisions of the leader or the leadership. Although it is often argued that this is a "biblical" structure of leadership, it is not a model of leadership that we see in Jesus. To be sure, Paul is not shy of correcting certain practices in the churches that he oversees, or of warning those who are conducting themselves in an ungodly manner. Out of love and friendship, and in humility, we can point out each other's weaknesses, and should be grateful when friends speak honestly to us. The idea that there are those who have a God-given right to wield authority over others in a church, however, is not something that appears in Jesus's teaching on leadership. In fact, the opposite is true. Those who lead are those who serve. Christian relationships are to be characterized by mutual submission, and not by one person dominating another. Christian leaders too must be open to correction, and in submission to others. Most human beings do not handle power and authority well, and if we spent more energy on being leaders who serve rather than leaders who dominate it might prevent some of the catastrophic "falls" that we witness among those who are given power and authority in the church.

DELIGHTING IN DIFFERENCE

Fifthly, good parents delight in their children's differences (from themselves and from their siblings). One of the joys of parenting is seeing the gifts and talents that our children have, and realizing that they are far more gifted than we are. Our children are gifted in ways that we are not. Another joy is to see siblings in the same family, each with their own unique personality. It is so true that no two people are alike! How do we end up so different from the people who were nurtured in the same home, and in the same way, as us? It is essential in church life to release ourselves, and others, from the notion of uniformity, and to encourage diversity. It is a key principle in the discipling of others—that we should encourage a great variety in the way that the life of Jesus is lived out through different individual lives around us.

What will be the impact of this on the younger generation or the ones we nurture? Grown-up children will inevitably form households and/or families of their own. In these new household units, they will retain some of the values of their parents (especially if they have valued their parenting), but they will also adapt and change as they come into contact with other influences outside their own families. Friends, husbands, wives, mentors, people who influence us throughout our lives will bring new values, new ways of doing things, new emphases, and new gifts into our lives. Parents are often astonished at how different their children are from them. This is why discipleship is best done as apprenticeship, and not as programs. Wisdom is passed on from one person to another, one group to another, and as it is passed on, it is incarnated in different ways. New communities will be subject to other influences. They will make alliances with different movements and different theologies. They will adopt different practices, liturgies, and styles. All this is part of healthy growth and good leaders will rejoice in the difference, rather than bemoaning the break from the past, or being threatened by difference. As parents, we never know what our children's families or households will look like, but we do know that they will look different from ours. Sometimes this can feel undermining. Sometimes parents take this as an implied criticism. It might be, and it might not be, but it is something that all church leaders and parents have to face. We have to acknowledge this, allow it, and accept it with good grace.

DIVERSITY AND NOT UNIFORMITY

We began by discussing the fact that diversity is essential in the Christian life, but in fact, it is essential in all life. When we dwell on the truth that we have a creator who has created a breathtakingly diverse universe, we cannot think otherwise. The sheer abundance of variety in the created world is amazing: the innumerable variety of species in the animal and plant kingdom; thousands of languages and cultures; different expressions of art and music; differences in personalities, facial expressions, gifting, relationships, siblings, and all things human. Heterogeneity is God-given and an integral part of existence. The church should be a place where this diversity is celebrated and not extinguished, all in the context of unity. This is the work of the Spirit—to bring unity and diversity. We are united but we are not uniform. Paul writes of this in relation to what it means to be the "body of Christ" (1 Cor 12). The work of the same Spirit and the same Lord gives rise to a multiplicity of gifts within the church, all given for the building up of the body. The Spirit unifies, but at the same time, anoints the creativity and the possibilities that arise from difference.

Unity is achieved through Christ and the Spirit. We are all called to be like the one Christ. To that extent, there is only one standard by which to measure the fullness of human existence and the wholeness of human being: Christ is the prototype of humanity—he is the pattern. This pattern, however, is not a thing that can be "copied" or applied to individuals in a uniform way. The Spirit is able to transform humanity into Christlikeness without extinguishing the uniqueness of the particular. We all live in different cultures, we have different backgrounds, gifting, personalities, and hundreds of different factors that make us into unique creations. For this reason, we become like Jesus in as many ways as there are human beings. This is why we must not think that we have to conform to one pattern of being a follower of Jesus over another.

TEACHING AND MODELING VALUES

Good parents impart values by teaching them *and* modeling them. The old adage of "do as I say, and not as I do" is amusing but has no credibility in the Christian life. The values that stay with us from our parental homes, or from the parental figures in our lives (carers, grandparents, teachers, pastors), are all values that we have seen lived out by someone to good effect.

We cannot force people, least of all our children, to accept our values. We can only impart values as best we can. If we are people who can impart values by living them out with integrity, then we will be invited to act as guides and friends for years to come. Good parents continue to act as guides, mentors, and friends throughout a child's life. It is true, that when children are young, they do not need their parents to be their friends, they need them to be their parents. Grown-up children, however, often count their parents as their "friends," and very often turn to them for advice and help if the relationship that has been built up is one of love and trust.

If we are fortunate we will have parents we can turn to for advice throughout our whole lives. We value their opinions because they know us so well, and we have a deep sense of familiarity and history. If we have been involved at any time in the apprenticeship of others, and have built up a relationship of trust and love which is at the same time releasing and empowering then those whom we have apprenticed will continue to relate to us for years to come. What we then find is that as the years go by we turn to those we have mentored for *their* advice and wisdom. In my own family, I have been humbled to see my parents turn to their children (or even grandchildren) when they need something from them, whether it is an expert, or a younger, stronger pair of arms, or a point of view. We start learning from our children the moment they are born. Parents do not know everything. A younger generation always has things to teach an older generation, and this is also true of spiritual truths. Insight and revelation come to people regardless of age, status, or gender. We all have much to learn from one another. Humility and a willingness to learn are an essential part of a culture in which the older generation releases the younger.

HAVING THE RIGHT ATTITUDE

In summary, nurturing and training others is a practice that all Christians should be involved in in some form. There are good books and good courses to help us along the way, but in reality this is most effective when we live alongside each other and open up our lives, our homes, and our relationships to one another. We are given to one another to teach each other to "do whatever he tells us to do." And to do this, not because we have to, but because we love to: because we have become convinced that following him is the way of freedom.

eight

A Present Future Hope

WE BEGAN WITH THE truth that following Jesus and trusting in him means that one day we will all be like him, and not only this, but this transformation is happening now, in this life we live on earth. However much we find it hard to believe that we are becoming like the Son, God is moving in us to bring this about. He has predestined our future: that we should reflect God's glory in our very beings. We will not just give glory to God, but we will *be* his crowning glory, because we will bear the image of his Son. Moreover, this dynamic of transformation by the Son and the Spirit is the means by which we will be set free to be who we were created to be. Sin binds us, constricts us, distorts us, and destroys us. The power of the death and resurrection of Christ releases us from the prison of sin, so that we are free to love God and to love one another. We are free to become a people who are shaped by our praise and worship of God. Placing God at the center of our lives in worship reorients us. We have a new center, which changes our values, our desires, and our relationships. "Now the Lord is the Spirit, and where the Spirit of the Lord is there is freedom. And we, who with unveiled faces all reflect the Lord's glory, are being transformed into his likeness with ever increasing glory, which comes from the Lord, who is the Spirit" (2 Cor 3:18).

Understanding that we are loved, restored, and forgiven while we are *still* sinners, means that we can extend love and forgiveness to others. It is only through God's extraordinary grace that we can be in his presence at all, and this is poured out because of his deep love of each one of us. As followers of Jesus, we are called to preach and to live out this message of freedom. We can become people who free one another, forgiving one another as we have been forgiven, extending mercy and releasing one another from the prisons that we inhabit. We are only able to do this through the power of the Word and the Spirit, but as a people who are in Christ, and in whom Christ dwells, we are given the gifts and the abilities to set one another free. We can do so in loving and encouraging speech, refusing to condemn one another. We can do so in giving time and value to another, listening to one another, and restoring dignity to one another. We can do so in our embrace and acceptance of one another. We can rejoice with one another, not begrudging another's successes, but delighting in each other's joys. We can pray for one another and offer companionship in times of suffering.

THE COAL AND THE DIAMOND

Changing the way that we think and act happens over time. This is why we so often feel discouraged and hopeless, because we feel we take two steps forward and one step back—or even two steps back! God is very patient, and he works over time, sometimes taking far more time than we can bear. If this life is just the beginning of an eternal life, then we probably really have no idea of the meaning of time. What feels like an age to us is just a fleeting moment in God's economy. I know that the illustration of the coal to diamonds is an old one, but it is also a rich one. I love the fact that diamonds are made out of coal. It is difficult to imagine that something as beautiful as a diamond has its origins in something as unimpressive as a lump of coal. Diamonds and coal are both forms of carbon, but they have different structures, hence their radically different appearances. Coal is not pure carbon; it is also full of decomposed plant and animal material—impurities. Over millions of years, and under extreme pressure, these impurities are purged from the coal as it is formed into graphite. Again under extreme pressure and heat, diamonds are then formed from the graphite deep inside the earth, and carried near to the earth's surface by molten magma. Graphite and diamonds look so extraordinarily different because of the arrangement of the atoms, but the point is that *they are both made of the same "stuff."* Human beings are being transformed like coal to diamonds. We already have what we need to become like Jesus because we have been created in his image. It is out of who we are already that we will be made new. Over time, and sometimes under extreme pressure, the impurities are purged and we are formed and re-formed into something unspeakably beautiful.

THE CROSS AND THE KINGDOM

There is one particular and crucial teaching of Jesus's on discipleship that I could have begun with, but I have chosen to end with. Jesus said this to his disciples:

> If anyone would come after me, he must deny himself and take up his cross daily and follow me. For whoever wants to save his life will lose it, but whoever loses his life for me will save it. What good is it for a man to gain the whole world, and yet lose or forfeit his very self? If anyone is ashamed of me and my words, the Son of Man will be ashamed of him when he comes in his glory and in the glory of the Father and of the holy angels. (Luke 9:23–26)

At the heart of the Christian life is a strange paradox. We are called to give up our lives, sometimes literally to do so, just as Christ gave up his own life, and in doing so, we gain an eternal, fulfilled, joyful, and blessed life. In fact, the *only* way to gain this life is to give up our own lives to him. Taking up our crosses daily, and dying to ourselves sounds hard, painful, and sacrificial. It is. And yet, Jesus also teaches that if we come to him and take his yoke upon us and learn from him that his burden will be easy, his yoke will be light, and we will find rest for our souls (Matt 11:25–30). How can the cross we carry, which is hard and painful and sacrificial, be an easy burden and light yoke?

Later in Matthew, Jesus teaches on the nature of God's kingdom. "The kingdom of heaven is like treasure hidden in a field. When a man found it, he hid it again, and then in his joy went and sold all he had and bought that field." And, "Again, the kingdom of heaven is like a merchant looking for fine pearls. When he found one of great value, he went away and sold everything he had and bought it" (Matt 13:44–46).

The kingdom of heaven is something of infinite worth but only gained by great sacrifice. In both parables, the men sell everything they own for this treasure. They lay down everything to gain the kingdom.

I imagine that to so many people, being a Christian seems so unimpressive, but I often think it takes great courage to be a Christian. It takes courage to be different and apparently foolish. It takes courage to declare

God's goodness in the face of extreme suffering. It takes courage to submit our wills and our desires to God, and to love one another in ways that make us feel vulnerable and exposed. It takes courage to give up worldly wealth and acclaim. It takes courage to risk offering the good news about Jesus, prayer for healing, a prophetic word. God promises us that the life of faith and trust in Jesus Christ will be one of power and strength, but the path to this power is through weakness. This is the way of the cross.

The process of relinquishing our wills and our desires to God, and taking up his will and his desires is a painful and sacrificial road. Nobody is able to do this easily. When the Son came to earth in the life of Jesus, he chose to live his life in the way that we live ours. In each moment, Jesus submitted and conformed his human will to the divine will. In Gethsemane, we see the extreme suffering that he underwent to be obedient to the Father, but he did this "for the joy set before him." Living in God's kingdom means living in a strange, inverted world. We get glimpses of the unseen reality that we live with, which convinces us all over again that the sacrifices are more than worth it. What we have given up in order to live the life of faith is so small and pathetic compared to what we are being given. The more we "die" to ourselves, the more the glory and the power of God will be made manifest in us and through us. Paul writes this, "If we died with him, we will also live with him; if we endure, we will also reign with him" (2 Tim 2:11–12). The work of the kingdom is often unseen: it is like the yeast that works through a whole batch of dough; it is like the seeds under the ground that will one day spring up into beautiful plants; it is like the wind that blows but we cannot see where it comes from or where it is going. Taking part in God's kingdom sometimes feels like being part of a resistance movement that works underground. It is not overtly powerful. It is subversive, costly, and thrilling all at the same time.

FOLLOW ME . . .

Jesus calls us to follow him, and this means following him wherever he leads us. It means "following" in so many different ways. We follow him like we follow a dance partner. We follow his teachings. We follow the leading of the Spirit. We follow in his footsteps to the cross. We follow his example in loving the outcast, praying for the sick, and delivering those who are oppressed by demons. We follow him because he has won us: by his love and his beauty, his power and grace, his truth and forgiveness. We find, even in the worst times, that we refuse to follow anyone else, because only he has the words of eternal life. But nobody ever follows perfectly. Learning to follow Jesus is a personal journey and it takes a lifetime.

In John 21 Jesus appears to the disciples by the Sea of Tiberius. They have been fishing all night and have caught nothing. Jesus calls to them and tells them to throw their net on the right side of the boat. They do so, and haul in a huge catch of fish. As soon as that happens, Peter knows that he is in the presence of the Lord. He strips off and jumps into the water, swimming to shore to get to Jesus. When they had finished eating, Peter and Jesus have a poignant and somewhat heartrending exchange. Three times Jesus asks Peter if he loves him. Three times Peter replies, "Yes, I do love you; you know I love you." He is hurt at being asked three times over. After the third time, Jesus gives Peter a hard word, "'when you are old you will stretch out your hands, and someone else will dress you and lead you where you do not want to go.' Jesus said this to indicate the kind of death by which Peter would glorify God." Then he says to Peter, "Follow me." At this moment, Peter does what so many of us would have done. He looks over his shoulder at John and he asks, "What about him?" Jesus replies, "If I want him to remain alive until I return, what is that to you? You must follow me."

It is so easy to compare one life with another. It is so natural to say to Jesus, "What about him? What about her?" Why do I take this path and she takes that one? Why does following Jesus look great for some people and so hard for others? There are no real answers to that question. Jesus just replies, "What is that to you? Follow me." We cannot really compare our journeys. It is God who chooses our paths and directs us in them. As much as we all look over our shoulders at those who walk with us, Jesus is always drawing our gaze back to him. We complain, and struggle and fail at following him. We delude ourselves into thinking it would be easier if this or that could happen, if life was different, if the people around us were easier, but Jesus's steady call just continues, "Follow me." When my children were small, and they were being fractious and difficult, I would mostly be fractious and difficult back, but in my better moments, I knew that what I needed to do was to remain calm, and to calm them down too. Sometimes, when I needed them to listen to me, I would crouch down in front of them, take their faces into my hands, turn their heads towards me, and draw their gaze to mine. Jesus always turns our faces towards him. When he came to this earth in Christ, God knelt down before us so that we could see him. We will constantly be tempted to look over our shoulder, but instead, we need to let God turn our faces towards him, to stop looking over our shoulders, and to fix our eyes upon Jesus. The life of faith is only possible because of the one who lived a life of unwavering faith. He is constantly faithful where we are faithless. He is unendingly trustworthy. Through *his* faithfulness, we are given the courage and the trust to follow him, even though we are faltering and fickle. God knows this. Jesus endured the cross for the joy set before him. The joy set before him is us. He scorned its shame in order to set us free and to live with us forever. He is now sitting at the right hand of the throne of God, where one day, we too will reign with him—in perfect freedom—and this life of perfect freedom has already begun.

Appendix

The Holy Habit of Fasting

Throughout the book, I have referred on a number of occasions to the fact that Jesus teaches in Matthew on three holy habits: prayer, fasting, and giving to the needy. In Matthew 6:16–18, Jesus refers to the practice of fasting, implying that it will be something his followers will do, just as they will pray and give to the poor. It appears that there is no question, really, that fasting is something Christians will engage in, although people constantly tell me they rarely hear much teaching on it. In this appendix, I wish to give some reasons why we should fast, to look at what might be happening when we do fast, and then to give some practical suggestions on how to go about it.

The first good reason to fast, then, is because Jesus himself fasts and, moreover, he assumes his followers will also. He teaches that when we fast, it should be a private affair, and that our outward appearance should be as it always is in everyday life. We should not fast to impress others. There is no doubt that fasting is a sacrifice, but Jesus also speaks of the "rewards" of fasting. The rewards of fasting are like the yield or benefits of fasting. We will clearly reap some benefit if we give to God in this way. The Gospels have a number of references to fasting. Jesus fasted in the desert for forty days before he is tempted by the devil. Jesus's response to why his disciples do not fast is recorded in all three Synoptic Gospels (Matt 9:14–17; Mark 2:18–22; Luke 5:33–39). Jesus tells the Pharisees that when he is gone, *then* his disciples will fast. Luke mentions the fasting of Anna in Luke 2:37 and the parable of the Pharisee who fasts in Luke 18:9–14. All three Synoptic Gospels tell the story of a boy with an evil spirit, whose father asks the disciples to pray. On praying for the boy, the disciples are unable to cast out the spirit, and when Jesus arrives, he rebukes them for their lack of faith. When they ask why he was able to do what they were not, Jesus replies that this kind only comes out by prayer. Some manuscripts add "and fasting" (Mark 9:29). Isaiah warns of fasting that is not accompanied by acts of giving to the poor, integrity, and justice (Isa 58). There are clearly right ways and wrong ways of fasting.

I have often wondered exactly why Jesus might have told the disciples that they could have prayed more effectively for the boy if they had been fasting. It sounds very strange to Protestant ears. Do we have to try harder to get results from God? Is there some performance on our part that will get a better result? This is one of the dangers of teaching on fasting. It can sound as if we are saying, the more fervent we become, the more God will deliver what we want. This is not true. We are not demonstrating how holy we are in order to get rewards, neither are we twisting God's arm. It is not a hunger strike! It is not clear what Jesus might have meant by telling his disciples that if they had fasted and prayed they might have prayed more effectively. However, I think there may be a number of factors involved. First, when we pray, fast, and study Scripture in humility, we will be developing our skill of discernment, of learning how God works in different situations, and following him. We will better discern "the spirits"—whether we feel a spirit behind a certain comment or behavior is genuinely godly or not. We will be developing our "tracking" skills. These practices will also strengthen our faith in God's ability to do all things, as we will be reminding ourselves that nothing is impossible with God. We will be connecting with the power of the Spirit in prayer, and thus perceiving the spiritual world with greater clarity. I believe that these are some of the benefits or "rewards" of fasting that Jesus is talking about in Matthew 6.

Fasting has long been a practice in the church, and is carried out in many different ways from total fasting (water only) to partial fasting (either eating simply or giving up one particular type of food or drink for an extended period of time). What is fasting? Why do we do it? And what do we achieve by it?

WHAT IS FASTING?

Although it has become common for people to say that they are "fasting" from particular pastimes or activities, such as Facebook, the internet, games consoles, TV, etc., the type of fasting I will focus on here is the practice of fasting from food. This is the fasting mentioned in the Bible, the word being linked to physical "hunger." When we fast from food, we are hungry, and there is something in experiencing this hunger that is crucial for the dynamic of prayer with fasting, which I will go on to explain. There is also something about fasting from food that encompasses all aspects and principles of fasting, in a way that the other forms of fasting do not. So here, when I am talking about fasting, I mean choosing to forego food, or most foods, for a period of time, that period being anything from a few hours to a period of days or even weeks. We undoubtedly need food to live, but we do not need an enormous amount of food in the way that we need water, for example, to survive. We may not *want* to go without food, but we are physically able to function on no food, or very little food, even for extended periods. Jesus fasted for forty days in the desert, and I have heard that this is a maximum time recommended for fasting. I know that there are people who have fasted for longer than this, but I personally have not known anyone who has done that, so I do not feel able to comment on this, neither would I recommend it.

WHY FAST?

There are numerous reasons for fasting, both practical and spiritual, that deepen our relationship with God, our prayer lives, our ability to hear from God, and our ability to follow the leading of the Spirit. Firstly, there is the simple dynamic of releasing time in our day to spend on prayer, Bible study, and worship. By giving up time preparing, eating, and washing up food, we put aside *this* to focus on *that*. (Obviously, this does not apply if we still have to spend time cooking for others, but even then, it might free up some time for prayer.) Secondly, we are denying ourselves some of the comforts of life, which has certain spiritual and emotional benefits. We are all tempted to fill up certain needs that we have with "things." Human beings are always seeking comfort in the material and physical aspects of life, some of which are healthy, and some of which are not. Moreover, we can all easily fall into excess with the things that comfort us if we do not learn to exercise self-control. When we fast, we deny ourselves the physical comfort of food, which we do not need for a while, in order to focus or to "feast" on the Lord. As we do so, there are a number of important dynamics going on in our bodies and minds. First of all, we will experience hunger, and to some extent, deprivation. This may sound extreme, but it is amazing how quickly we begin to feel deprived if we cannot have what we want when we want. As we decide, over the day (or days) to continue to refuse to give in to our cravings and longings for food, meat, sugary foods, or whatever we have decided to give up, we find our need for that particular comfort begins to fade. It has less of a grip on us. By doing this, we are exercising self-control and discipline in one particular area of life. This will then help us to exercise self-control in other aspects of life, whether that is in relation to drinking, video games, anger, sexual temptation, or the like. Fasting from food will help us to be generally self-controlled, and this is a great basis for a fruitful life with God.

Thirdly, we de-clutter our minds. Fasting is a good way of bringing a sense of focus to our minds. If we are specifically fasting for one or two situations, the fact that we are hungry all day means that our minds go back continuously to the thing we are praying for. Fourthly, fasting can be cleansing. Cutting out certain foods or drinks can be cleansing for the body. Many people just in general will fast (or detox) for this reason. Fasting in the Bible is sometimes linked to penitence or repentance. It is a good practice when we are fasting to begin the day with a time of confession and repentance. Fifthly, fasting is a way of bringing our wills more closely into line with God's will. The fact that we are making a significant sacrifice for a time in order to pray helps us become more yielding to God. We pray the prayer that Jesus prayed in Gethsemane more effectively—not my will but yours. We are making time for God, we are spending time in confession and repentance, we are exercising self-control, and we are submitting our wills to his in prayer. We relinquish our own desires for food, and this helps us to be prepared to relinquish our own desires for other things. At the same time, we begin to desire the things that God desires. We starve one desire in order to feed another. It is all these aspects of fasting that allow us to hear with more clarity from God when we fast, to connect with the Spirit and the power of God, and to be more prepared to do what he says. So on what occasions should we fast?

WHEN TO FAST

Years ago, I heard David Parker teach on fasting and he described it as "a disciplined expression of mourning." When people mourn, they are too sad to eat. They are mourning the loss of someone precious and experiencing the pain of longing for that person to be restored to them, even if they know it is now impossible. We grieve the loss of loved ones, whether they have died, or whether they have just moved a long way away from us. In chapter 5, I described the process of realizing what God's kingdom brings, and then longing for that to happen. When we are fasting, we are expressing the mourning and longing to see God's kingdom come and to see evidences of his presence in particular situations. We are longing to see his kingdom come, and for his will to be done. So we fast when we are seeking God for something in prayer and we want to be able to express that longing. I think of fasting on these occasions as if we are saying to God, this is more important to me than that. It is like weeping in prayer. There is no point in crocodile tears, because God knows the thoughts of our hearts, but when we are genuinely moved to weep in prayer, like Jesus wept and cried out, we do so because we are deeply moved and engaged in a situation. We feel compassion for those we are praying for. Jesus felt compassion for those he healed. For all these reasons, the occasions on which I would recommend fasting would be the following:

1) When we are faced with a particularly intractable problem and we are longing for a spiritual breakthrough.

2) When we sense that we are in the middle of a "battle." (Jesus fasted in the desert before he was tempted by Satan, and he was prepared for the battle that he faced.)

3) When starting a new venture or moving into a new ministry. When we are facing important decisions.

4) When we are appointing anyone to a position or a new ministry. The early church is recorded as fasting in Acts 13:2 and 14:23. While they were worshipping the Lord, and fasting, the Holy Spirit speaks to the gathered congregation leading them and guiding them as to what to do, both in sending out Paul and Barnabas, and in the appointment of elders in the church.

5) When we are praying for conversions.

6) When our children or loved ones are facing difficulties and hardships. If we have children, I think that one of the greatest gifts we can give to our children is to pray and to fast for them, especially when they are facing hardships and difficulties. The same goes for any family members or friends.

7) When we are in a conflict with someone and we need to repent, forgive, and seek forgiveness.

HOW DO WE FAST?

The rule for fasting is the same as the rule for praying, "fast as you can, and not as you can't." If you suffer from various health conditions, you will not be able to take part in any form of total fasting: asthmatics, diabetics, anorexics, and anyone with an illness where you need food regularly must not fast in any drastic way. This does not mean that we cannot make significant sacrifices, which I will mention below. If you know you can fast, but you are not sure where to begin, I would start very simply. We had a group of young people once who we were mentoring, and we had done some teaching on fasting. One of the girls was very open with us all about the fact that the idea of going without food was absolutely awful for her, and she just could not imagine doing it. Apart from loving the fact that she had a healthy love of food, we also wanted to encourage her that even a little bit of fasting might be a blessing to her. I think we must have said something to that effect. The next time we met, she had had a go. On one day, she had decided that she would skip breakfast, and she had gone a whole morning without food up until lunchtime, making more time in her morning for prayer. This made me smile, as some people never eat breakfast anyway, but for her this was a real sacrifice, and it made a huge difference. It genuinely had not been easy for her, but in the morning she had set aside time for prayer and really reaped the benefits. She was excited about her newfound world. We do not always have to do without food completely. I remember one time when I was pregnant and looking after three small children, wanting to join some of our church in a fast, but feeling I really could not do without food. Instead of fasting from food, I gave up tea, which meant that I did not have my morning cup of tea to help me get up, and I drank cold water instead. It sounds so pathetic, but I missed my tea all morning. I had a hunger for tea, which the water could not reach, and it reminded me all morning to pray for the situation that we were praying for at that time.

So first, fast as you can and not as you can't. Secondly, never compare your fast with anyone else's. It is not a competition as to who can live on less for longer! If you start a fast, and you just cannot carry on for any reason, give up without feeling guilty, and try again another time. I rarely fast totally. I never felt comfortable driving children around, for example, if I was lightheaded. I would eat fruit, drink fruit juice, or have a smoothie. You could have a slice of bread, a bowl of soup, or something light and frugal that does not necessarily fill you up, but stops you from collapsing. If you want to go without food completely, and just have water, I would highly recommend giving up tea and coffee a couple of days beforehand. If you are a tea and coffee drinker and you give up food and caffeine all at once, you will have a terrible headache by mid-morning, and it will be a real distraction from prayer. Other tips include planning a fast so that you do not have a busy day ahead of you, and fasting and praying with others to hear what God is saying. It can be so encouraging to fast with a group, and then to pray together, and to hear that many of you were sensing God directing your prayers in the same way.

I feel that I am just at the beginning of learning what prayer is all about, and the fasts that I undertake are genuinely very, very small, but whenever we hear stories of others who have fasted and prayed it gives me such encouragement to carry on. As I said in the beginning, however, it is not a holiness competition. We give out of what we have, and the only person we need to be conscious of is God. There is much about this process of fasting that I feel I cannot explain, except that I know that it works. Jesus talks about the rewards of prayer and fasting, and the rewards can only really be experienced, but it is yet another gift from God for engaging in the life of his kingdom and co-laboring with him in this world.

Bibliography

Allen, Roland. *Missionary Methods: St. Paul's or Ours?* Grand Rapids: Eerdmans, 1962.
———. *The Spontaneous Expansion of the Church.* Eugene, OR: Wipf and Stock, 1962.
Aquinas, Thomas. *The Summa Theologica of St. Thomas Aquinas.* 2nd ed. 1920. Translated by Fathers of the English Dominican Province. Copyright 2009 by Kevin Knight. Online: www.newadvent.org/summa/
Bailey, Kenneth. *Jesus through Middle Eastern Eyes: Cultural Studies in the Gospels.* London: SPCK, 2008.
Benedict XVI. "*Lectio Divina* on John 15." (2010) Pontifical Roman Major Seminary.
Calvin, John. *Institutes of the Christian Religion.* Translated by Henry Beveridge. Peabody, MA: Hendrickson, 2008.
Chadwick, Samuel. *The Path of Prayer.* Kansas City: Beacon Hill, 1931.
Cole, Neil. *Organic Church: Growing Faith Where Life Happens.* San Francisco: Jossey-Bass, 2005.
Davidson, Ivor. "Theologizing the Human Jesus: An Ancient (and Modern) Approach to Christology Reassessed." *International Journal of Systematic Theology* 3.2 (2001) 129–53.
Donovan, Vincent. *Christianity Rediscovered: An Epistle from the Masai.* London: SCM, 1989.
Ferguson, S. B., and David F. Wright, editors. *New Dictionary of Theology.* Leicester, UK: InterVarsity, 1988.
Hughes, S., and Trevor J. Partridge. *Cover to Cover Complete: Through the Bible as It Happened.* Surrey, UK: CWR, 2007.
Louth, Andrew, editor. *The Apostolic Fathers: Early Christian Writings.* Translated by Maxwell Staniforth. London: Penguin, 1987.
Nouwen, Henri. *Words of Hope and Healing: Ninety-Nine Sayings by Henri Nouwen.* New York: New City, 2005.
Pelikan, J., and Helmut Lehmann, editors. *Luther's Works: American Edition.* 55 volumes. St. Louis: Concordia, 1955.
Rae, Murray. "Theological Interpretation and the Problem of Method." Unpublished paper, 2012.

Bibliography

Smail, Thomas. *The Giving Gift: The Holy Spirit in Person*. London: Hodder & Stoughton, 1988.

Vanhoozer, Kevin J. *The Drama of Doctrine: A Canonical Linguistic Approach to Christian Theology*. Louisville, KY: Westminster John Knox, 2005.

Willard, Dallas. *The Divine Conspiracy: Rediscovering Our Hidden Life in God*. London: Fount, 1998.

———. *The Great Omission: Reclaiming Jesus' Essential Teachings on Discipleship*. Oxford: Monarch, 2006.

Winner, Lauren. *Real Sex: The Naked Truth about Chastity*. Grand Rapids: Brazos, 2005.

Lightning Source UK Ltd.
Milton Keynes UK
UKOW040304071212

203272UK00001B/19/P